Architecting a Framework for Edge AI Functional and Non-functional Requirements

RIVER PUBLISHERS SERIES IN COMMUNICATIONS AND NETWORKING

The "River Publishers Series in Communications and Networking" is a series of comprehensive academic and professional books which focus on communication and network systems. Topics range from the theory and use of systems involving all terminals, computers, and information processors to wired and wireless networks and network layouts, protocols, architectures, and implementations. Also covered are developments stemming from new market demands in systems, products, and technologies such as personal communications services, multimedia systems, enterprise networks, and optical communications.

The series includes research monographs, edited volumes, handbooks and textbooks, providing professionals, researchers, educators, and advanced students in the field with an invaluable insight into the latest research and developments.

Topics included in this series include:

- Communication theory
- Multimedia systems
- Network architecture
- Optical communications
- Personal communication services
- Telecoms networks
- Wifi network protocols

For a list of other books in this series, visit www.riverpublishers.com

Architecting a Framework for Edge AI Functional and Non-functional Requirements

Editors

Ovidiu Vermesan

SINTEF, Norway

Alain Pagani

DFKI - German Research Center for Artificial Intelligence, Germany

River Publishers

Routledge
Taylor & Francis Group
NEW YORK AND LONDON

Published 2026 by River Publishers
River Publishers
Broagervej 10, 9260 Gistrup, Denmark
www.riverpublishers.com

Distributed exclusively by Routledge
605 Third Avenue, New York, NY 10017, USA
4 Park Square, Milton Park, Abingdon, Oxon OX14 4RN

Architecting a Framework for Edge AI Functional and Non-functional Requirements / by Ovidiu Vermesan, Alain Pagani.

Routledge is an imprint of the Taylor & Francis Group, an informa business

ISBN 978-87-4380-957-9 (hardback)
ISBN 978-87-4380-959-3 (online)
ISBN 978-87-4380-958-6 (master ebook)
ISBN 978-87-4380-961-6 (ePub)

DOI: 10.1201/9788743809586

Contents

Preface

The rise of edge AI systems is transforming industries by enabling real-time decision-making, reducing latency, and enhancing privacy. From autonomous vehicles and robotics to industrial automation and personalised healthcare, the applications of edge AI are advancing and growing. The unique characteristics of edge AI systems, which operate at the intersection of hardware, software, AI technology stack, and data, present a complex set of challenges in ensuring their performance, dependability and trust.

This book provides a comprehensive exploration of the functional and non-functional requirements that are critical to the design, development, and deployment of dependable and trustworthy edge AI systems. It offers a system perspective that spans the entire edge continuum, from the micro-edge of embedded sensors to the deep-edge of gateways and the meta-edge of on-premises high-performance servers where edge and cloud computing meet. The book delves into the intricate relationship between a system's operational requirements and its ability to perform as expected, a concept defined as dependability. In the context of real-time edge AI systems, dependability is the assurance that services can be trusted to function correctly within specified time constraints.

Building on this foundation, the book introduces the concept of trustworthiness as the verifiable fulfilment of both functional and non-functional requirements. A trustworthy edge AI system is one whose correctness can be rigorously checked whether by human experts or automated tools. Achieving this level of trust is a technical challenge and a collaborative endeavour that requires a synthesis of technical precision, ethical considerations, and legal and regulatory compliance.

Throughout this book, the authors argue that trustworthy edge AI systems are developed through a continuous process of defining requirements, setting key performance indicators (KPIs), and implementing robust monitoring and assessment.

This book is structured based on engineering principles to guide the reader through the multifaceted landscape of edge AI systems. The book begins with an introduction to the fundamental concepts and a taxonomy of terminology. The next chapter moves into the specifics of edge AI system engineering, followed by dedicated chapters on both non-functional and functional requirements. Recognising the broader context in which these systems operate, the book addresses the general legal requirements and industry standards that are pertinent to their design and development. Finally, the book concludes with a synthesis of the key insights, offering a forward-looking perspective on the future of dependable and trustworthy edge AI based on systems and requirements engineering principles applied to functional and non-functional requirements of these systems.

List of Figures

List of Tables

List of Contributors

Vermesan, Ovidiu, *SINTEF, Norway*

Pagani, Alain, *DFKI, Germany*

Belkadi, Lydia, *KU Leuven, Belgium*

Bahr, Roy, *SINTEF, Norway*

Cano, José, *University of Glasgow, UK*

Selim, Mohamed, *DFKI, Germany*

Kozanitis, Christos, *FORTH, Greece*

Pazos, Nuria, *HES-SO, Switzerland*

Romano, Martina, *SCM Group, Italy*

Beysens, Jona, *KU Leuven, Belgium*

de Prado, Miguel, *VERSES, Switzerland*

Vállez Enano, Noelia, *University of Castilla-La Mancha, Spain*

Déniz Suárez, Óscar, *University of Castilla-La Mancha, Spain*

Capotondi, Alessandro, *UNIMORE, Italy*

Pau, Danilo, *STMicroelectronics, Italy*

Urlini, Giulio, *STMicroelectronics, Italy*

Al Koutayni, Mhd Rashed, *DFKI, Germany*

Crowley, Elliot J., *University of Edinburgh, UK*

Diana, Francesco, *INRIA, France*

Giroire, Frederic, *INRIA, France*

Hynes, Jacqueline, *VERSES, UK*

Neglia, Giovanni, *INRIA, France*

Paudel, Danda, *Sofia University, Bulgaria*

Tutschku, Kurt, *Blekinge Institute of Technology, Sweden*

Van, Gool Luc, *ETH, Switzerland*

Xu, Chuan, *INRIA, France*

List of Abbreviations

ADR	AI, Data and Robotics
AI	Artificial Intelligence
AIA	Artificial Intelligence Act
AI-aaS	AI-as-a-Service
AIMS	AI Management System
AINN	AI-Native for Telecommunication Network
AI RMF	AI Risk Management Framework
AIS	Autonomous Intelligent System
AI4N	AI for Networks
API	Application Programming Interfaces
ASIC	Application-Specific Integrated Circuit
BAS	Building Automation System
B2B	Business-to-Business
B2C	Business-to-Consumer
B2G	Business-to-Government
CAD	Computer Aided Design
CEN	European Committee for Standardization
CENELEC	European Committee for Electrotechnical Standardization
CMMI	Capability Maturity Model Integration
CNN	Convolutional Neural Network
CPU	Central Processing Unit
CSA	Coordination and Support Action
DID	Decentralised Identifier
DL	Deep Learning
DSP	Digital Signal Processor
DVFS	Dynamic Voltage and Frequency Scaling
EC	European Commission
ECPAIS	Ethics Certification Program for Autonomous and Intelligent Systems

EDIH	European Digital Innovation Hub
EDPB	European Data Protection Board
EIC	European Innovation Council
EIF	European Investment Fund
EoT	Eyes of Things
ESOs	European Standards Organisations
ETSI	European Telecommunications Standards Institute
EU	European Union
FAIR	Findable, Accessible, Interoperable and Reusable
FG	Focus Group
FPGA	Field-Programmable Gate Array
FPS	Frames per Second
FR	Functional Requirement
FSTP	Financial Support to Third Parties
GDPR	General Data Protection Regulation
GPAI	General Purpose AI
GPU	Graphical Processing Unit
hENs	Harmonised European Standards
HSM	HW Security Module
HSML	Hyperspatial Modelling Language
HSTP	Hyperspatial Transaction Protocol
HVAC	Heating, Ventilation and Air Conditioning
HW	Hardware
IDS	Intrusion Detection System
IEC	International Electrotechnical Commission; Intelligent Edge Computing
IEEE	Institute of Electrical and Electronics Engineers
INCOSE	International Council on Systems Engineering
IoT	Internet of Things
IP	Intellectual Property
ISA	Instruction Set Architecture
ISO	International Organization for Standardization
ISP	Image Signal Processor
ISS	International Space Station
ITU-T	International Telecommunication Union - Telecommunication Standardization Sector
JPL	Jet Propulsion Laboratory
JTC	Joint Technical Committee

KPI	Key Performance Indicator
LIME	Local Interpretable Model-agnostic Explanations
LLM	Large Language Model
LSTM	Long Short-Term Memory
MAP	Mean Average-Precision
MCU	Microcontroller Unit
MEC	Multi-access Edge Computing
mIoU	Mean Intersection over Union
ML	Machine Learning
MOOC	Massive Open Online Course
MSE	Mean-Square-Error
MTBF	Mean Time Between Failures
NAS	Neural Architecture Search
NASA	National Aeronautics and Space Administration
NFR	Non-Functional Requirement
NIST	National Institute of Standards and Technology (U.S.)
NLP	Natural Language Processing
NN	Neural Network
NoE	Network of Excellence
NPU	Neural Processing Unit
ODM	Original Design Manufacturer
OECD	Organisation for Economic Co-operation and Development
OEM	Original Equipment Manufacturer
OS	Operating System
OSHW	Open Source Hardware
OSHWA	Open Source Hardware Association
OSI	Open Source Initiative
PGD	Projected Gradient Descent
PLC	Programmable Logic Controller
PSNR	Peak Signal-to-Noise Ratio
QMS	Quality Management System
RAM	Random Access Memory
R-CNN	Region-based CNN
RE	Requirement Engineering
RGB	Red, Green, Blue (colour system)
RISC	Reduced Instruction Set Computer
RNN	Recurrent Neural Network

SA	Standard Association
SC	Subcommittee
SCADA	Supervisory control and data acquisition
SDK	Software Development Kit
SDOs	Standards Development Organisations
SG	Study Group
SHAP	Shapley Addictive Explanations
SMART	Specific, Measurable, Achievable, Relevant, and Time-bound
SME	Small and Medium Enterprise
SoC	System on Chip
SoM	System on Module
SOTA	State-of-the-Art
SQuaRE	System and software Quality Requirements and Evaluation
SRA	Strategic Research Agenda
SSD	Single Shot Detector
SSMA	SQL Server Migration Assistant
SW	Software
SWIDs	Spatial Web Identifiers
TC	Technical Committee
TDP	Thermal Design power
TDW	Theme Development Workshop
TEE	Trusted Execution Environment
TEF	Testing and Experimentation Facility
TPU	Tensor Processing Unit
TRL	Technology Readiness Level
UDG	Universal Domain Graph
V&V	Verification and Validation
VEC	Vehicular Edge Computing
VPU	Vision Processing Unit
W3C	World Wide Web Consortium
XAI	Explainable edge AI
XR	Extended Reality

1

Introduction and Background

On the global market, several nations are racing to achieve a global innovation advantage in AI as it is understood that AI is a foundational technology that can boost competitiveness, increase productivity, protect national security, and help solve societal challenges. Comparing China, the European Union, and the United States in terms of their relative standing in the AI economy by examining six categories of metrics: talent, research, development, adoption, data, and hardware, the United States leads in absolute terms, with China coming in second, and the European Union lags further behind. This order could change in the coming years depending on a range of policy actions that can propel each nation or region to improve its AI capabilities [11, 14]. AI technology developments significantly impact electronic and component systems, semiconductor design, and production, as the amount of data processed and stored by AI applications continues to increase. Semiconductor architectural improvements are needed to address data use in AI-integrated circuits, and improvements in semiconductor design for AI are requested to enhance overall performance, speed, memory capacity, with increased energy efficiency. In this context, major initiatives have started globally to address the development of the semiconductor industry, such as the European Chips Act, which aims to bolster Europe's competitiveness, resilience, and help achieve both the digital and green transition [12]. In this context, edge AI represents a paradigm shift in deploying and utilising AI technologies, marking a transformative evolution from centralised data processing systems to decentralised, edge-oriented solutions. The edge AI deployments are characterised by massive scale and heterogeneity. A single system may comprise many devices with diverse hardware and software stacks, creating significant challenges for deployment, interoperability, and management. These devices are often deployed in uncontrolled environments, making them vulnerable

DOI: 10.1201/9788743809586-1

to physical tampering and environmental hazards, which introduces a class of security threats not typically considered in secure data centres. This tightly coupled system of trade-offs, forced by a resource-scarce environment, makes a holistic systems engineering approach a must.

This transition underscores the capability of executing AI algorithms directly on intelligent edge devices and embedded systems across the edge continuum, including micro-, deep- and meta-edge, including avoiding the need for constant connectivity to cloud-based processing centres. As edge AI is developed and applied across various sectors, understanding the edge AI system's functional and non-functional requirements becomes imperative to harness the full potential of technology.

Edge AI refers to the deployment of AI algorithms, machine learning (ML), deep learning (DL) and generative AI models directly on local, interconnected edge devices, such as Internet of Things (IoT) devices, smartphones, security cameras, gateways, embedded systems and on-premises servers using edge computing processing. By processing data locally, edge AI systems can deliver real-time analytics and decision-making with significantly reduced latency, which is critical for applications like autonomous vehicles and industrial automation. This approach enhances data privacy and security by minimising the transmission of potentially sensitive information to the cloud, reduces the demand for network bandwidth and associated costs, and enables operational autonomy in environments with intermittent or non-existent network connectivity.

The design of edge AI systems is fundamentally constraint-driven. These constraints are not minor implementation details but are the primary architectural drivers that shape every design decision. The most prominent is the severe limitation on resources. Edge devices are typically constrained by processing power, available memory (RAM and flash storage), and, most critically, energy consumption, which directly impacts battery life and thermal management.

These resource limitations impose direct constraints on the AI models themselves. Large, complex models are not appropriate at the edge, which necessitates the use of lightweight model architectures and aggressive model compression techniques, such as quantisation (reducing the precision of model weights), pruning (removing unnecessary connections), and knowledge distillation (training a smaller "student" model to mimic a larger "teacher" model). While on-device training offers benefits for privacy and adaptation to new data, it is exceptionally challenging due to these same resource constraints.

Edge AI systems must also contend with network constraints. Although they are designed to operate with less reliance on the cloud, they are not entirely disconnected. The need for model updates, data synchronisation, or federated learning means that systems must be robust to environments with limited, unreliable, or costly network connectivity.

The rapid integration of AI and edge AI into various sectors has moved the technology from a research area to a driving force of digital transformation.

The technical, market and social developments in automation and integration of AI in industrial environments advance the topic of ethics of AI, dependability combined with industrial AI trust, which focuses on achieving the desired outcome for AI-based technologies and applications in various industrial sectors while complying with legal rules and adhering to ethical norms. Addressing the complex interrelation between ethics and AI comes with notable dynamics, controversial issues, a lack of standards and no common agreement on principles about ethics. In addition, trust in AI and edge AI systems has multiple dimensions combining system dependability characteristics (e.g., privacy, security, safety, reliability, availability, resilience, connectability and maintainability) with human and machine behaviour, which require a greater understanding of how individuals interact with machines and how machines/things interact with other machines/things to extend trust [70].

In these conditions, technology companies are focused on building AI platforms that meet the stakeholders' needs for optimised performance, profitability and security. In doing so, they are partnering across the AI ecosystem of semiconductor and integrated circuits companies, hyperscalers, large language models, data and software companies, and engaging with global trade policy unknowns and resource constraints. The trends in new AI frontiers and the focus on companies in these environments include AI reasoning, custom silicon, edge and cloud balanced migrations, systems to measure AI efficacy and building an agentic AI future [15].

These transitions and trends necessitate a structured approach to governance and technical oversight, which is the primary role of standardisation and regulations. Standards provide a common language and a set of established principles for developing, deploying, and maintaining AI and edge AI systems. They are crucial for ensuring that AI technologies are not only innovative but also safe, secure, reliable, and aligned with societal values [7, 115].

Regulatory bodies are increasingly looking to standards as a means to ensure compliance and manage the complexities introduced by AI

[115, 145]. For instance, the European Union's AI Act [6, 115, 129] references harmonised standards as a mechanism for demonstrating conformity with its legal requirements.

Similarly, initiatives like the U.S. National Institute of Standards and Technology (NIST) AI Risk Management Framework (AI RMF) provide guidance that is being adopted and referenced by organisations globally [8]. This synergy between regulation and standardisation is creating a framework for responsible AI innovation, pushing developers and organisations to adopt best practices in their AI engineering [131] disciplines.

A global ecosystem of standardisation bodies is actively working to address the multifaceted challenges of AI and edge AI. Each organisation brings a unique perspective and expertise, contributing to a holistic standards landscape. Their collaborative efforts are essential for avoiding fragmentation in standardisation activities and ensuring that standards are globally relevant and applicable across diverse industries and use cases. Fragmentation in standardisation activities refers to the situation where the lack of coordination or agreement can lead to multiple, competing standards, hindering the benefits of standardisation such as interoperability and market efficiency. As a result, this can display as diverging national or regional standards, or even within the same sector or industry, creating a fragmented landscape that can be costly and complex to navigate.

The proliferation of AI and edge AI has created an urgent need to move beyond research-oriented development towards a more disciplined, engineering-focused approach. The concepts of AI and edge AI engineering [131] have emerged to meet this need, advocating for the application of established principles from systems engineering, software engineering [130], requirements engineering and human-centred design to construct AI and edge AI systems that are functional, reliable, secure, and aligned with human values and mission objectives.

This evolution from experimental development to robust engineering is occurring in parallel with, and is significantly influenced by, the global push for regulation. Governments and international bodies are grappling with the societal, ethical, and economic implications of AI, leading to landmark legislative efforts. The adoption of the Artificial Intelligence Act (AIA) by the European Union in June 2024 introduced the first horizontal rules addressing the risks to health, safety and fundamental rights posed by AI systems. The AI Act framework categorises AI systems by risk as illustrated in Figure 1.1 and imposes stringent requirements on those deemed "high-risk" [115, 6].

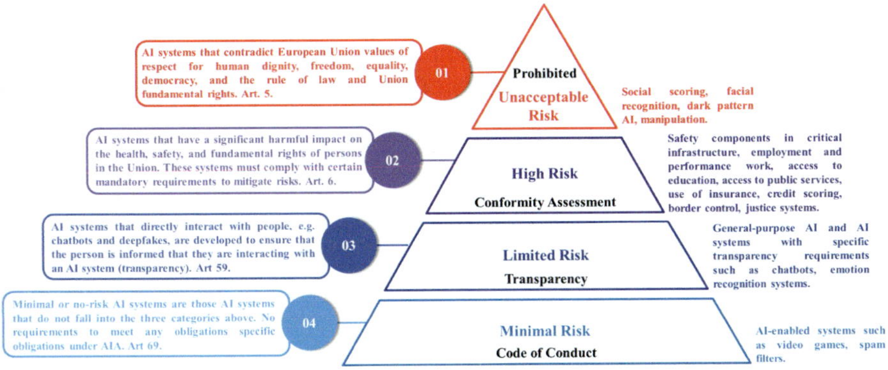

Figure 1.1 The EU AIA' pyramid of risks.

Most AI systems and applications pose minimal or no risks. Specific AI systems are subjected to transparency obligations, e.g., when they interact with natural persons or pose risks of impersonation or deception. High-risk AI systems are limited to those that could have a significant, harmful impact on the health, safety, or fundamental rights of individuals. For these, the AIA defines a clear set of requirements, as extensively discussed in this document. The AIA regulation prohibits certain AI practices that pose unacceptable risks [144].

The AIA provides for the development of harmonised European standards ('hENs') to address these risks. Adhesion to these standards by AI providers will facilitate conformity assessments and provide a presumption of compliance with all or parts of the AI Act's requirements, to be assessed on a case-by-case basis.

The legislation empowers European Standards Organisations (ESOs) to develop these harmonised standards, which, when used by developers, provide a "presumption of conformity" with the law's technical requirement [9].

AI standardisation remains voluntary, also under the AIA. The market-driven nature of standardisation and differ depending on ESOs internal organisation (i.e., industry representation vs. national representation). The linkage between law and technical specification is transforming the AI and edge AI standardisation and can influence the market access.

The result is a dynamic and complex global standardisation landscape, where multiple Standards Development Organisations (SDOs) are working to create the necessary frameworks, guidelines, and technical specifications.

This report provides an exhaustive overview of these efforts, analysing the work of the International Organization for Standardization (ISO), the International Electrotechnical Commission (IEC), the Institute of Electrical and Electronics Engineers (IEEE), the International Telecommunication Union - Telecommunication Standardization Sector (ITU-T), the European Telecommunications Standards Institute (ETSI), and the European Committee for Standardization (CEN) and European Committee for Electrotechnical Standardization (CENELEC). Each organisation brings a unique perspective and focus, contributing distinct yet complementary pieces to the global puzzle of AI governance.

This book aims to structure and explain the comprehensive set of requirements essential for the successful realisation of edge AI systems.

Requirements in edge AI systems are classified into functional requirements (FRs), which define the functionality that the system must offer or what the system should do, and non-functional requirements (NFRs), known as quality requirements, that represent the desired qualities of the system, how well it should perform its functions, and include aspects like performance, reliability, and security. Constraints are pre-existing limitations on the design or development process, use of specific technology or standard, that cannot be influenced by the engineering design.

The book defines the functional and non-functional requirements and provides examples of their KPIs, measures (quantitative, qualitative), monitoring, ongoing assessment, transparency, and alignment with societal values and needs.

The FRs discussed address the core features, capabilities and tasks that edge AI systems perform to fulfil their intended purpose. These capabilities are critical considering the performance, latency, bandwidth, response times, energy efficiency, data processing, machine learning and deep learning model execution and real-time decision-making at the edge.

The NFRs focus on edge AI systems' quality attributes or characteristics that impact the performance. Topics such as functional suitability, performance efficiency, compatibility, interaction capability, reliability, security, maintainability, flexibility and safety are analysed to provide a holistic view of what is needed to ensure that edge AI systems can operate effectively in diverse and often constrained environments.

The book links the definition of functional and non-functional requirements of edge AI systems with the concepts of edge AI system dependability and trustworthiness.

Dependability is essential to the performance [20] of real-time edge AI systems and reflects edge AI systems' operational requirements while reflecting the degree of trustworthiness in the system. As a result, trustworthiness is the ability of an edge AI system to meet functional and non-functional requirements in a verifiable way, meaning that it can be checked for correctness by a person or tool through verification, validation, testing, and benchmarking and supported by explainability and interpretability methods [72].

By delineating and analysing the FRs and NFRs requirements, this book provides stakeholders, including researchers, designers, developers, system architects, and decision-makers, with a framework for designing and implementing edge AI solutions that meet operational objectives while delivering sustained value and efficiency. As we delve into the specifics of these requirements, the analysis highlights the challenges and opportunities associated with deploying AI at the edge yet guiding efforts to leverage this transformative technology in real-world applications.

2

Taxonomy and Terminology

The objective of this section is to provide an overview of taxonomy, terminology and definitions of AI and edge AI terms and concepts, which are essential for clear communication, systematic analysis, development of a strategic research agenda, innovation, regulation, business strategy, interdisciplinary collaboration, effective deployment and standardisation. It lays the foundation for the coherent and unified progress of the field.

Having standard definitions and terminology for AI and edge AI terms and concepts prevents miscommunications and misinterpretations arising from varying interpretations of terms, establishing a common baseline for discussions and ensuring that the stakeholders involved have a clear understanding of the key concepts.

Taxonomy allows the classification of different AI and edge AI methods, algorithms, and systems, making it easier to address and analyse them systematically by helping in effectively evaluating, comparing, and benchmarking different approaches, technologies, solutions, and applications.

A clear taxonomy can support identifying gaps in current research and areas that need further exploration and provide a solid foundation upon which new ideas, models, and technologies can be built.

Using a common taxonomy, terminology and definitions of AI and edge AI terms and concepts helps regulators and policymakers create appropriate frameworks, guidelines, and standards to ensure the ethical and safe development and deployment of AI and edge AI technologies, ensuring compliance and responsible AI deployment.

Edge AI applied to different industrial domains requires interdisciplinary collaboration, as the technology's development intersects with various fields, such as the Internet of Things (IoT), sensing/actuating, edge computing, cybersecurity, and intelligent connectivity.

Understanding the definitions and taxonomy can help identify the most suitable AI or edge AI techniques for specific real-world applications, optimise performance, and ensure practical feasibility.

DOI: 10.1201/9788743809586-2

2.1 Definitions

In this section, we propose definitions for the main concepts related to AI and edge AI considering that the challenge with a definition is that it specifies the meaning or significance of a word or phrase and can concern either its usage or the content of a concept expressed by a word.

Definition challenges often arise due to the inherent complexity and variability of the scientific and technological domain, as well as the different terminologies used in other domains.

Moreover, as technology and science evolve, so do their terminology and definitions, resulting in shifts in meaning that can render previously clear definitions outdated or incomplete. This dynamic nature of terminology requires continuous adaptation and consensus, which can be challenging to achieve across the scientific and industrial domains, especially in rapidly advancing or inherently subjective fields, such as AI technology.

2.1.1 Artificial Intelligence

Many AI researchers acknowledge that defining intelligence in a universally satisfactory manner is challenging. However, for the field to advance coherently, it is essential to reason from a clear and generally accepted statement of its subject matter. Despite the lack of a standardised definition of intelligence in AI today, establishing a common framework is crucial for guiding research, fostering communication, and ensuring consistent progress in the discipline.

In this context, several definitions of artificial intelligence and machine intelligence exist as listed in Table 2.1.

AI system: An AI system is a machine-based system that, for explicit or implicit objectives, infers from the input it receives, how to generate outputs such as predictions, content, recommendations, or decisions that can influence physical or virtual environments. Different AI systems vary in their levels of autonomy and adaptiveness after deployment [81].

ISO/IEC DIS 22989 standard defines an AI system as an engineered system featuring AI. The AI systems can be designed to generate outputs such as predictions, recommendations and classifications for a given set of human defined objectives. The AI systems can be designed to operate with varying levels of automation [21].

AIA states that an AI system means a machine-based system that is designed to operate with varying levels of autonomy and that may exhibit adaptiveness after deployment, and as mentioned above, for explicit or

Table 2.1 AI definitions

Definition
• Artificial intelligence is that activity devoted to making machines intelligent, and intelligence is that quality that enables an entity to function appropriately and with foresight in its environment [67].
• The study of agents that receive percepts from the environment and perform actions [68].
• The science of making machines do things that would require intelligence if done by humans [61].
• The use of computer programs and programming techniques to cast light on the principles of intelligence in general and human thought in particular [61].
• Artificial Intelligence is a science and a set of computational technologies that are by inspired by-but typically operate quite differently from-the ways people use their nervous systems and bodies to sense, learn, reason, and take action [64].
• Intelligence is the capacity of an information-processing system to adapt to its environment while operating with insufficient knowledge and resources [74].
• Artificial Intelligence is a fully controlled agent with a capacity of an information-processing system to adapt to its environment while operating with insufficient knowledge and resources [73].
• Artificial intelligence may be considered a computational construct, as it is inferred from the outcomes of simulated aspects of human thought and decision-making, which are facilitated by data processing, machine learning techniques, and algorithmic principles [62].
• Intelligence is the computational part of the ability to achieve goals. A goal achieving system is one that is more usefully understood in terms of outcomes than in terms of mechanisms [65].
• Artificial intelligence is a machine's ability to perform logical analysis, acquire knowledge, and adapt to an industrial environment that varies over time or in context. These abilities include the collective attributes of a machine (i.e., computer, robot, or intelligent IoT device) to perform functions such as perception, understanding, reason, prediction, learning, decision making and action [2].
• Artificial intelligence is the discipline of research and development of mechanisms and applications of AI systems. Research and development can take place across any number of fields such as computer science, data science, humanities, mathematics and natural sciences [21].
• Artificial intelligence refers to systems that display intelligent behaviour by analysing their environment and taking actions – with some degree of autonomy – to achieve specific goals. AI-based systems can be purely software-based, acting in the virtual world (e.g., voice assistants, image analysis software, search engines, speech and face recognition systems), or AI can be embedded in hardware devices (e.g., advanced robots, autonomous vehicles, drones or Internet of Things (IoT) applications) [10, 16, 17, 18].
• Engineered system set of methods or automated entities that together build, optimize and apply a model so that the system can, for a given set of predefined tasks, compute predictions, recommendations, or decisions [21].
• Discipline study of theories, mechanisms, developments and applications related to artificial intelligence engineered system [21].

Table 2.1 *Continued.*

Definition
• AI is a fast-evolving family of technologies that contributes to a wide array of economic, environmental and societal benefits across the entire spectrum of industries and social activities. By improving prediction, optimising operations and resource allocation, and personalising digital solutions available for individuals and organisations, the use of AI can provide key competitive advantages to undertakings and support socially and environmentally beneficial outcomes, for example in healthcare, agriculture, food safety, education and training, media, sports, culture, infrastructure management, energy, transport and logistics, public services, security, justice, resource and energy efficiency, environmental monitoring, the conservation and restoration of biodiversity and ecosystems and climate change mitigation and adaptation [116].

implicit objectives, infers from the input it receives, how to generate outputs such as predictions, content, recommendations, or decisions that can influence physical or virtual environments [116].

AI training: Is defined as the process to determine or to improve the parameters of a machine learning model, based on a machine learning algorithm, by using training data [21].

AI inference: Reasoning by which conclusions are derived from known premises. A premise is either a fact, a rule, a model, a feature or raw data [21].

The edge AI definition builds on the converge of AI, IoT and edge computing technologies and is defined later in this section. It is useful to note that in continual learning, training and inference stages are no longer purely subsequent, but more heavily intertwined.

2.1.2 Open-Source

Open source is a paradigm and practice that promotes the free access, use, and modification of software, hardware, or other resources. It emphasises collaboration, transparency, and community-driven development. Open source typically involves distributing the source code or design files, allowing users to study, modify, and improve the product. This approach fosters innovation and inclusivity, enabling diverse contributions and widespread adoption.

Open-source hardware centres on making physical design files and documentation available for replication and modification. Open-source software focuses on freely accessible source code and the ability to modify and redistribute software. Open-source AI involves sharing code, models, and datasets for collaborative advancement, emphasising ethical considerations and transparency.

The most widely recognised definitions of open-source are the ones provided by the Open Source Initiative (OSI) [87], which maintains a set of criteria for what constitutes open-source software and now open-source, and the Open Source Hardware Association (OSHWA) [88] which maintains the definition and set of standards for open-source hardware.

The AI and edge AI developers are supporting open-source developments, and the European Commission is increasingly reinforcing the open accessibility of research outputs, including data, code, hardware and publications [83]. This push is part of the broader Open Science policy, aiming to make research more transparent, efficient, and impactful. Open access promotes better science and innovation in both public and private sectors. The Open Research Europe platform provides guidelines for authors on managing and sharing their research data [84]. These guidelines emphasise the importance of making data openly accessible and reusable. This European platform endorses the **FAIR** principles that emphasise making data **F**indable, **A**ccessible, **I**nteroperable and **R**eusable [85].

Open-source Hardware:

The OSHWA provides a widely recognized definition and set of standards for open-source hardware [88]. The definition is based on the Open Source Definition for Open Source Software [87].

Open Source Hardware (OSHW) refers to tangible artifacts, such as machines, devices, or other physical things, whose design has been released to the public so that anyone can make, modify, distribute, and use it. This definition aims to provide guidelines for developing and evaluating licenses for OSHW.

Hardware differs from software in that physical resources must always be committed to creating physical goods. Therefore, individuals or companies producing items ("products") under an OSHW license have an obligation to make it clear that such products are not manufactured, sold, warrantied, or otherwise sanctioned by the original designer and not to make use of any trademarks owned by the original designer.

The distribution terms of OSHW must comply with the following criteria [88]:

- **Documentation -** The hardware must be released with documentation including design files and must allow modification and distribution of the design files. Where documentation is not furnished with the physical product, there must be a well-publicized means of obtaining this documentation for no more than a reasonable reproduction cost, preferably downloading via the Internet without charge. The documentation must include design files in the preferred format for making changes, such as the native file format of a CAD program. Deliberately obfuscated design files are not allowed. The license may require that the design files are provided in fully documented, open format(s).

- **Scope -** The hardware documentation must clearly specify what portion of the design, if not all, is being released under the license.
- **Necessary Software -** If the licensed design requires software, embedded or otherwise, to operate properly and fulfil its essential functions, then the license may require that one of the following conditions be met:
    - The interfaces are sufficiently documented that it could reasonably be considered straightforward to write open-source software that allows the device to operate properly and fulfil its essential functions. For example, this may include using detailed signal timing diagrams or pseudocode to clearly illustrate the interface in operation.
    - The necessary software is released under an OSI-approved open-source license.
- **Derived Works -** The license shall allow modifications and derived works to be distributed under the same terms as the license of the original work. The license shall also allow for the manufacture, sale, distribution, and use of products created from the design files, the design files themselves, and derivatives thereof.
- **Free redistribution -** The license shall not restrict any party from selling or giving away the project documentation. It shall not require a royalty or other fee for such sale or for the sale of derived works.
- **Attribution -** The license may require derived documents and copyright notices associated with devices to provide attribution to the licensors when distributing design files, manufactured products, and/or derivatives thereof. The license may require that this information be accessible to the end-user using the device typically but shall not specify a specific format of display. The license may require derived works to carry a different name or version number from the original design.
- **No Discrimination Against Persons or Groups -** The license must not discriminate against any person or group of persons.

- **No Discrimination Against Fields of Endeavor -** The license must not restrict anyone from using the work (including manufactured hardware) in a specific field of endeavour. For example, it must not restrict the hardware from being used in a business or from being used in nuclear research.
- **Distribution of License -** The rights granted by the license must apply to all to whom the work is redistributed without the need for execution of an additional license by those parties.
- **License Must Not Be Specific to a Product -** The rights granted by the license must not depend on the licensed work being part of a particular product. If a portion is extracted from a work and used or distributed within the terms of the license, all parties to whom that work is redistributed should have the same rights as those that are granted for the original work.
- **License Must Not Restrict Other Hardware or Software -** License Must Not Restrict Other Hardware or Software: The license must not place restrictions on other items that are aggregated with the licensed work but not derivative of it. For example, the license must not insist that all other hardware sold with the licensed item be open-source, nor that only open-source software be used external to the device.
- **License Must Be Technology-Neutral -** License Must Be Technology-Neutral: No license provision may be predicated on any individual technology, specific part, or component.

On the hardware side, RISC-V plays a crucial role in the open-source movement [13, 103]. RISC-V is an open standard Instruction Set Architecture (ISA) which allows anyone to design and sell RISC-V-based chips without licensing fees, fostering innovation and competition. Its flexibility and customizability make it suitable for various applications, from embedded systems to high-performance computing and AI. This inclusivity makes it easier for smaller companies to enter the market and encourages the use of open-source hardware, allowing high-performance computing to become available to a larger audience. Other open-source hardware platforms for AI are:

- **BeagleBone** [104]: An open-source development board that offers a powerful platform for AI and machine learning applications.
- **Raspberry Pi** [105]: The Raspberry Pi is a low-cost, credit-card-sized computer that can be used for a variety of AI projects. Its affordability and versatility make it an excellent choice for hobbyists and educators

looking to explore AI. Although the Raspberry Pi itself is not entirely open-source, its schematics are regularly released as documentation, and it does support and contribute to the open-source community.

- **ESP32** [106]: The core ESP32 hardware, developed by Espressif Systems, is proprietary. However, there are open-source hardware versions available, such as the ESP32-EVB by Olimex.
- **Antmicro's Open-Source Jetson Baseboard** [107]: There are open-source projects and community contributions that enhance the Jetson ecosystem. Antmicro has developed an open-source Jetson baseboard to allow customers to get full control of the solutions that we build based on it, along with unmatched flexibility, transparency and usability.
- **Eyes of Things (EoT) Project** [102]: The schematics of the EoT board were made public on the project's website. However, the main blocks, like the Myriad processor, were not disclosed.

Open-source Software:

According to the Open-Source Initiative, open-source software must comply with the following criteria:

- **Free Redistribution:** The software can be freely distributed to anyone without restrictions, including both source code and compiled binaries.
- **Source Code:** The source code must be included or made available, allowing users to modify and improve the software.
- **Modification:** Users must be able to modify the software to suit their needs. This includes the ability to create derivative works.
- **Integrity of the Author's Source Code:** Distributions of modified versions may be allowed only if they are clearly marked and not misrepresented as the original software.
- **Non-Discrimination Against Persons or Groups:** The license must not discriminate against any person or group of persons.
- **Non-Discrimination Against Fields of Endeavor:** The license must not restrict anyone from using the software in a specific field of endeavour, such as business or research.
- **Distribution of License:** The rights attached to the software must apply to all who receive it, making it unnecessary to sign further agreements.
- **License Must Not Be Specific to a Product:** The rights attached to the software must not depend on the software being part of a particular product.
- **The License Must Not Restrict Other Software:** The license should not impose restrictions on other software distributed along with the open-source software.

- **Technology-Neutral:** No provision of the license may be predicated on any individual technology or style of interface.

Open-source software is built on several key principles:

- **Collaboration:** Open source encourages collaborative development, allowing developers from different backgrounds to contribute to and improve the software.
- **Transparency:** With access to source code, users can understand how the software operates, which fosters trust and accountability.
- **Community-Driven:** Open-source projects often rely on communities of users and developers who advocate for improvements and support one another.
- **Innovation:** Open-source promotes innovation by allowing anyone to build upon existing software, leading to rapid development cycles and diverse applications.
- **Access and Inclusion:** By removing cost barriers and restrictions, open-source software is accessible to a wide range of users, including those in developing countries.

These principles help to create a dynamic ecosystem where software can evolve and adapt to meet the needs of its users while promoting inclusivity and collaboration.

Open-source AI:

The potential and the critical challenges of open-source AI are highlighted in several references [86, 89, 92, 93]. On the positive side, open-source AI can enhance transparency and facilitate the auditing of AI systems, which in turn can build citizen trust. It also stimulates economic activities and fosters domain-specific expertise by allowing both the public and private sectors to innovate more freely. However, legal challenges arise from the need to navigate complex intellectual property rights and licensing issues. Another drawback is that maintaining and updating AI projects can be demanding, requiring substantial resources and expertise. Data-related challenges include ensuring the availability of high-quality datasets and addressing privacy concerns. Risk management is another critical area, as open-source AI systems can be more vulnerable to security threats. Additionally, societal and ethical challenges must be considered, such as the potential for bias in AI systems and the broader implications of AI deployment on society.

Open-source hardware and software have revolutionized the field of AI, making advanced technologies more accessible and fostering innovation through community collaboration. Thus, we can claim that it is not only the advent of deep learning and powerful GPUs what have caused the AI explosion, but also the widespread access to research results, code and datasets. An open-source AI ecosystem has helped lower the barriers for researchers, students and practitioners to acquire AI skills and develop prototypes of new exciting ideas. Some well-known examples of open-source software for AI include:

- **TensorFlow and PyTorch** [94, 95]: Developed by Google and Facebook's AI Research lab respectively, they are two of the most prominent open-source frameworks for AI. They offer a comprehensive ecosystem of tools, libraries, and community resources that support a large variety of AI applications.
- **Keras** [96]: Keras is a high-level neural networks API, written in Python and capable of running on top of TensorFlow, Microsoft Cognitive Toolkit, Theano, or PlaidML. It allows for easy and fast prototyping, making it a popular choice for beginners and experts alike.
- **Hugging Face** [97]: It is known for its open-source contributions. The company provides a suite of tools, including the popular Transformers library, which offers pre-trained models for tasks such as text classification, translation, and summarization. Hugging Face's commitment to open-source AI is evident in its extensive model hub, where developers can share and access a wide range of models and datasets.
- **OpenCV** [98]: It is one of the most well-known and widely used computer vision libraries in the world. Its extensive collection of algorithms and tools makes it a go-to choose for both beginners and experts in the field of computer vision. Since OpenCV 3.1 there is DNN module in the library that implements inferencing with deep AI networks, facilitating the integration of AI solutions in computer vision applications.
- **Gymnasium** [99]: Gymnasium is an open-source Python library for developing and comparing reinforcement learning algorithms by providing a standard API to communicate between learning algorithms and environments, as well as a standard set of environments compliant with that API. Gymnasium is a fork of OpenAI's Gym library.
- **NVIDIA Jetson open-source components** [100]: Although the hardware is proprietary, some tools and libraries associated with Jetson are open-source. For example, jetson-stats is an open-source package for monitoring and controlling Jetson devices.
- **PYNQ** [101]: An open-source project from Xilinx that makes it easy to design embedded systems with Python and programmable logic.

- **Eyes of Things (EoT) Project** [102]: EoT was an Innovation Action funded under the European Union's H2020 Framework Programme that built an open embedded computer vision platform with AI capabilities. The generated code was made public at the end of the project.
- **Lightweight Kubernetes (K3s):** K3s is a certified lightweight Kubernetes distribution that automates application software deployment to edge AI devices.

Within the ongoing AI arms race (present almost every day in mass media), big companies are eager to get traction and publicity via open sourcing part of their work. Independent of this, the open-source paradigm can indeed be profitable within the field of AI. Take for example the case of company OpenAI, which started with the explicit aim to develop open and safe artificial intelligence for humanity. A few years later, however, OpenAI transitioned to a capped-profit model, citing the need for substantial funding and competitive advantage [108]. This shift highlights the tension between open-source ideals and the practical demands of sustaining advanced AI research and development. Balancing openness with financial viability remains a significant challenge in the AI industry.

However, what truly constitutes "open-source" in the context of AI remains an open question. Addressing this question is crucial because it impacts how AI technologies are developed, shared, and used globally. Key points of the discussion to define open-source AI are [86]:

- **Accessibility:** Open-source AI tools allow individuals and organizations with limited resources to experiment with and develop AI technologies.
- **Collaboration:** Open-source projects foster a collaborative environment where developers can share ideas, improve existing tools, and create innovative solutions.
- **Transparency:** Open-source software and hardware promote transparency, enabling users to understand how AI models work and ensuring that they can be audited for fairness and bias.
- **Customization:** Users can modify open-source tools to suit their specific needs, leading to more appropriate and effective AI solutions.
- **Cost-Effectiveness:** Open-source projects reduce the cost of development by providing free access to high-quality tools and resources.
- **Ethical and Legal Considerations:** This includes concerns about the misuse of AI technologies and the need for regulations to ensure responsible use.

The need for a specific definition of open-source AI arises from the unique characteristics of AI systems compared to traditional software. AI systems involve not just code, but also models, training data, and weights. Without a clear definition, some entities might misuse the term "open-source" for marketing purposes, leading to confusion and potentially undermining trust in AI technologies.

The Open source Initiative (OSI) has been working since mid-2023 to create a clear definition of open-source AI [89], based on OECD's definition of AI [81]. This involves ensuring that AI systems are transparent, modifiable, and shareable, adhering to the principles of open-source software. OSI has brought together researchers, lawyers, policymakers, activists, and representatives from major tech companies like Meta, Google, and Amazon [86]. Having a diverse group is essential to ensure that the definition is robust and widely accepted, helping to find a balance between different perspectives and interests [92].

The OSI's "Open-Source AI Definition" emphasises four fundamental freedoms [89]:

- **Freely Usable:** The AI components should be freely usable by anyone for any purpose.
- **Understandable:** Users need to know how AI systems were created and work.
- **Modifiable:** Users should be able to modify AI systems to suit their needs.
- **Shareable:** AI systems, with or without modifications, should be shareable with others, promoting further innovation and collaboration.

Additionally, AI systems require transparency regarding their training data, source code, and models, ensuring that researchers can inspect and understand the systems. This level of transparency is crucial for building trust in AI systems to reuse and modify them. To modify an AI system, the following needs to be considered [89]:

- **Data Information:** Detailed data information is required to recreate an AI system. This includes training methodologies, data sets, gathering process, scope, characteristics, selection process, labelling, and curating methods. Data must be available under licenses that comply with the Open-Source Definition.
- **Code:** Source code for training and running the AI system must be available with OSI-approved licenses.

- **Weights:** Model weights and parameters must be available under OSI-approved terms.

The current draft also makes a distinction between open-source AI models and weights. An AI model includes the architecture, parameters (weights), and inference code, while AI weights are the learned parameters that overlay the model architecture.

The convergence of open-source software and AI is driving rapid advancements in several different sectors. The open-source AI approach comes with high innovation potential, in both the public and private sector, thanks to the capacity and uptake of individuals and organisations to freely reuse the software under open-source licences. Advantages include the ability to enhance transparency, facilitate the auditing of AI and thereby enhance citizen trust, while stimulating economic activities and domain-specific expertise. Disadvantages and limits include legal, technical, data, risk management, societal and ethical challenges. Several open-source AI pro and cons are identified and seven recommendations to boost its uptake are proposed in [66].

2.1.3 Edge Computing

Edge computing is a distributed computing paradigm that brings computation and data storage closer to the location where they are needed to improve response times and save bandwidth. Edge computing processes data locally on or near the device that generated it, such as IoT devices, sensors, or local on-premises servers.

The key features of edge computing are the proximity to where the data is generated reducing latency and enabling faster processing, while providing bandwidth efficiency by reducing the amount of data that needs to be transmitted to a central data processing. This allows for real-time processing with minimal delays, scalable growth as devices and data volumes increase and enhanced security and privacy by keeping sensitive data closer to its source and controlling data flow to centralised systems. The following sub-sections provide the definitions and the descriptions of the concepts of micro-, deep- and meta-edge developed in [75, 76].

2.1.4 Micro-Edge

Micro-edge is defined as the miniaturised version of edge computing, implemented where the sensing/actuating computational resources and capabilities

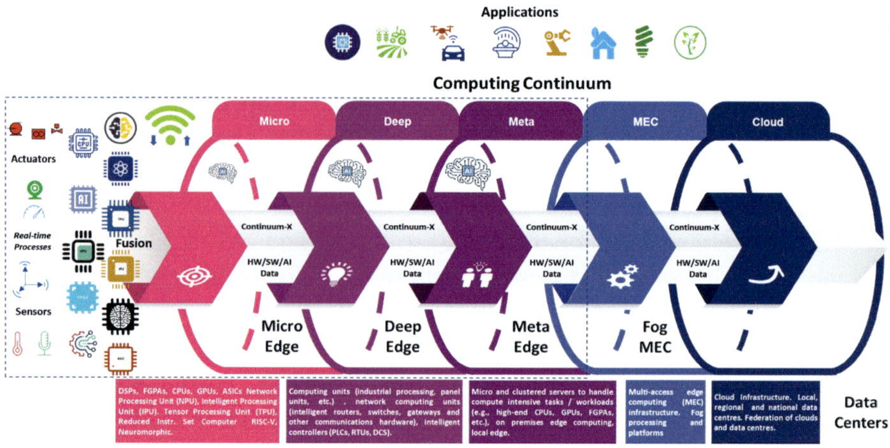

Figure 2.1 Edge granularity [75].

are deployed into microdevices. The concept pushes processing and analytics to be performed on micro, lightweight, and outer resource-constrained devices compared to single-board computers and gateways. These devices may distil information from the data collected by integrating AI-based algorithms for inference and training. Intelligent micro-edge allows real-time applications to become omnipresent and react quickly and intelligently to inferred situations while consuming minimal power.

The micro-edge includes intelligent sensors (physical, chemical, environmental parameters, perception, etc.) and actuators (audio, motion, etc.) systems with processing and connectivity capabilities that generate insight data and analytics. Micro-edge devices are implemented using microcontrollers built around ARM Cortex M0, M0+, M3, M4, M7X, ASICs and RISC-V. The distance from the data source (sensors/actuators) is minimised, and the micro-edge devices have extreme constraints on cost and power consumption [75, 76].

2.1.5 Deep-Edge

Deep-edge involves deploying advanced computational resources and AI capabilities at the edges of networks. The deep-edge model emphasises processing data in real-time, close to the data source, involving more complex computationally intensive applications than the micro-edge. Deep-edge devices have a higher power budget since they are shared across multiple endpoints and generally have a more capable processor which can be multiplexed to support those endpoints.

The deep-edge comprises intelligent controllers, PLCs, SCADA elements, connected machine vision systems, networking equipment, gateways, and computing units that aggregate data from the sensors/actuators and IoT devices. Deep-edge processing capabilities are implemented with performant processors and microcontrollers, such as Intel i-series, Atom, ARM Cortex M7+, etc., including CPUs, GPUs, TPUs, FPGAs and ASICs. The system architecture, including the deep-edge, relies on foreseen functionality and deployment options. These functions include cognitive capabilities that can acquire, aggregate, understand, react to data, exchange, and distribute information.

Deep-edge computing enables a new level of AI-driven analysis and autonomy at the extreme edges of networks, supporting the growing demand for responsive, intelligent, and decentralised data processing across various sectors [75, 76].

2.1.6 Meta-Edge

Meta-edge computing enables a high level of edge processing and AI-driven analysis on high performance processors and on-premises servers emphasising enhanced integration, scalability, and coordination across edge computing continuum. Meta-edge offers adaptability to changing conditions and requirements, such as fluctuating workloads, network conditions, or data flows, adjusting resource deployment and task execution accordingly while generating higher-level insights or decisions that require understanding or context from broader data sets.

The meta-edge integrates processing units, typically on-premises, implemented with high-performance embedded computing units, edge machine vision systems, and edge servers (e.g., high-performance CPUs, GPUs, FPGAs, etc.), which are designed to handle compute-intensive tasks (e.g., data series, image, and video processing), advanced analytics, AI-based functions, networking, and data storage.

Meta-edge aggregates data and insights from multiple edge nodes, creating a meta-level understanding or intelligence that can inform broader network or enterprise-level decisions [75, 76].

2.1.7 Edge AI

Edge AI combines AI, IoT and edge computing technologies and provides real-time collection, computing, and analytics, allowing data processing and execution of AI algorithms to occur directly on devices at the network's edge. By bringing AI closer to the source of data generation, edge AI enables more efficient and responsive decision-making in various applications.

Edge AI uses AI-based algorithms and techniques on edge devices, enabling more rapid and efficient data processing and improved privacy and security. Edge AI provides computational intelligence to develop intelligent systems that perform real-time tasks that typically require human-level intelligence, such as decision-making, problem-solving, pattern recognition, and learning.

By combining AI's analytical capabilities with the IoT's sensing/actuating capabilities, intelligent connectivity, and the distributed architecture of edge computing, edge AI offers robust, efficient, and secure solutions across diverse industries, supporting the growing demand for intelligent and autonomous systems.

2.1.8 Edge AI System Dependability

The International Electrotechnical Commission (IEC) addresses the dependability concept through the Technical Committee TC 56, which develops and maintains international standards. These standards provide systematic methods and tools for assessing and managing the dependability of equipment, services, and systems throughout their life cycles. Based on the vocabulary provided by IEC in this work, edge AI dependability is defined as the ability of the edge AI system to perform as and when required, operate as desired, and satisfy the defined functional and non-functional requirements. The term edge AI system dependability includes the core system's attributes and characteristics such as availability, connectability, maintainability, privacy, reliability, resilience, safety, security, to which AI specific attributes and characteristics are added, e.g., accountability, accuracy, authenticity, credibility, controllability, compliance, durability, efficiency, explainability fairness, inclusiveness, integrity, interpretability, interoperability, learnability, performance, robustness, transparency, understandability, usability.

The attributes and characteristics of edge AI system dependability can be expressed qualitatively or quantitatively through expressing the ability to perform by defining the functional and non-functional requirements in terms of features, functions and qualities to be performed, when the performance is to be achieved, considering operational conditions, the KPIs and measures specified.

Following the concept in [2, 5] a systematic structure of the concepts of edge AI dependability consists of three elements: attributes, threats, and means [4].

The attributes or characteristics are represented by the ways to assess the dependability of an edge AI system. These attributes or characteristics are qualities of an edge AI system. These can be assessed to determine its overall dependability by defined KPIs using qualitative or quantitative measures.

The threats are represented by the elements that can affect the dependability of an edge AI system (errors, failures, faults). An error is a discrepancy between an edge AI system's intended behaviour and actual behaviour inside the edge AI system boundary. Errors occur at runtime when some part of the edge AI system enters an unexpected state due to the activation of a fault. Errors are generated from invalid states and algorithms and are challenging to find without unique mechanisms. A failure is an instance in time when an edge AI system displays behaviour that is errant from its specification. An error may not necessarily cause a failure, but the edge AI system's performance is influenced. A fault is a defect in an edge AI system, and its presence may or may not lead to a failure due to input and state conditions that may never cause the fault to be executed so that an error occurs.

The means are represented by the ways to increase an edge AI system's dependability (forecasting, prevention, removal, tolerance) and are intended to reduce the number of failures made visible to the users of an edge AI system.

2.1.9 Edge AI System Trustworthiness

Trustworthy edge AI systems are essential for user confidence, the safe deployment of edge AI technologies including generative AI, and ensuring that these systems enhance technological, economic and societal progress.

According to [17], trustworthy AI should be lawful by respecting all applicable laws and regulations, ethical by respecting ethical principles and values, and robust from a technical perspective while considering its social environment. Trustworthy AI is dependent upon consistent and veracious application of these three underpinning principles from conception through to application [151].

The Dictionary.com defines "trustworthiness" as the quality of being deserving of trust or confidence, dependability. The National Institute of Standards and Technology (NIST) [19] defines "trustworthiness" as the following: "trustworthiness is the demonstrable likelihood that the system performs according to designed behaviour under any set of conditions as evidenced by characteristics including, but not limited to, safety, security, privacy, reliability and resilience. In computer security, a chain of trust is established by validating each component of hardware and software from the bottom up. It is intended to ensure that only trusted software and hardware can be used while still retaining some level of flexibility".

Based on the definition of trustworthiness in ISO/IEC TS 5723:2022 [42], edge AI trustworthiness can be defined as the ability of the edge AI system to meet the functional and non-functional requirements and user expectations in a verifiable way, which includes measurability and demonstrability by means of objective evidence that needs verification to ensure that user expectations are met. The verification process considers the definition of KPIs, measures, monitoring, ongoing assessment, transparency, and alignment with societal values and needs.

ISO/IEC TS 5723:2022 highlights that trustworthiness characteristics include accountability, accuracy, authenticity, availability, controllability, integrity, quality, reliability, privacy, resilience, robustness, safety, security, transparency, and usability.

Trustworthiness is an attribute that can be applied to edge AI systems and related services, products, technology, data and information.

ISO/IEC TR 24028:2020 [43] surveys topics related to trustworthiness in AI systems, including approaches to establish trust in AI systems through transparency, explainability, controllability, etc.; engineering pitfalls and typical associated threats and risks to AI systems, along with possible mitigation techniques and methods; and approaches to assess and achieve availability, resiliency, reliability, accuracy, safety, security and privacy of AI systems that can be applied as well to edge AI systems. The specification of levels of trustworthiness for AI systems is out of the scope of the document.

2.2 AI and Edge AI Taxonomy

The AI technology foundation has evolved over the years with the development of new technologies such as machine learning, deep learning, and generative AI, as illustrated in the Figure 2.2.

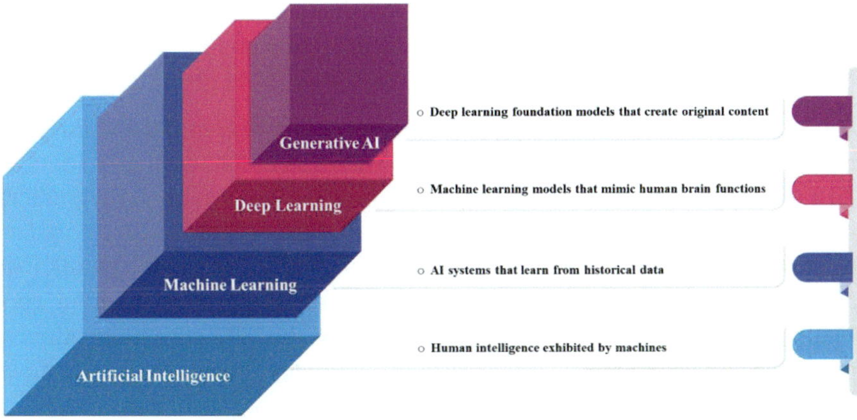

Figure 2.2 AI technology evolution.

Presenting a taxonomy and classification of AI and edge AI systems concepts is essential for understanding the landscape of edge deployments and defining the functional and non-functional requirements of such systems. These classifications guide the design of hardware, software, edge AI technology stacks, and datasets, and inform the strategic deployment of edge AI solutions across various industry domains. This helps maximise the potential of AI at the edge while addressing specific challenges and requirements of localised processing.

Creating a taxonomy and classification for edge AI systems involves categorising them based on various dimensions, including the specific AI and edge AI domains they serve. In this work, the concepts used are defined as follows:

Edge AI: is a distributed computing paradigm that integrates AI algorithms with IoT sensing and edge computing infrastructure to process data locally at the source where data is generated. Edge AI enables real-time analytics, intelligent decision-making, and enhanced privacy by executing computational tasks directly on edge devices rather than relying on centralised cloud connectivity. Edge AI can leverage generative and agentic AI to enable autonomous systems at the edge.

Machine Learning (ML): Edge AI domain that addresses the deployment of ML models optimised to fit edge devices with limited computational power, memory, and energy constraints. To maintain performance, this involves model compression techniques like quantisation, pruning, and distillation.

ML is defined in [21] as the process of optimising model parameters using computational techniques, such that the model's behaviour reflects the data or experience.

Distributed Machine Learning (DML): Execution of training and inference processes across multiple machines. Parallelisation can be applied to datasets and models [90, 91]. In dataset parallelism, each node computes gradients and local statistics on a subset of the original dataset. The resulting updates are subsequently aggregated by a parameter server. In model parallelism, each node trains a specific part of the model, with the central server coordinating the integration of the different components. By combining the two approaches, distributed machine learning facilitates the training of complex models on large datasets that would be infeasible on a single machine.

Deep Learning (DL): An edge AI domain that involves deploying deep learning models on edge devices. DL, a subset of ML, utilises neural networks with multiple layers (deep neural networks) to model complex patterns and representations in data. DL models perform inference directly on edge devices, enabling real-time data processing and decision-making. DL is an approach to creating rich hierarchical representations by training neural networks with many hidden layers. This process allows the neural network to progressively refine its final output. DL can reduce or eliminate the need for feature engineering, as the most relevant features are identified automatically. However, DL can require significant time and computing resources [21].

Natural Language Processing (NLP): Edge AI domain that handles human language data for applications such as voice recognition, language translation, and sentiment analysis on edge devices. NLP is defined in [21] as system information processing based upon natural language understanding defined in ISO/IEC 2382:2015 [170] as natural language comprehension extraction of information, by a functional unit, from text or speech communicated to it in a natural language, and the production of a description for both the given text or speech and what it represents or natural language generation defined as a task of converting data carrying semantics into natural language.

Supervised Learning: Edge AI domain that focuses on implementing supervised learning techniques directly on edge devices. Supervised learning is a type of ML where models are trained on labelled datasets, meaning the input data is paired with the correct output. This training enables models to make predictions or decisions when encountering new, unlabelled data. Supervised learning is defined in [21] and [41] as "machine learning that makes use of labelled data during training". In this context, ML models are trained with training data that include a known or determined output or target variable (the label). The value of the target variable for a given sample is also known as the ground truth. Depending on the task, labels can be of any type, including categorical, binary, or numeric values or structured objects (e.g., sequences, images, trees, or graphs). Labels can be part of the original dataset, but in many cases, they are determined manually or through other processes. Supervised learning can be used for classification and regression tasks, as well as for more complex structured prediction tasks [21].

Unsupervised Learning: Edge AI domain that focuses on implementing unsupervised learning techniques directly on edge devices. Unsupervised learning is a type of ML that infers patterns from unlabelled data, where the edge AI system learns the underlying structure without explicit output guidance. These systems can adapt to input data in real time, updating models as they encounter new patterns. Unsupervised ML is defined in [21, 41] as "machine learning that makes use of unlabelled data during training". Unsupervised ML can be useful in cases such as clustering, where the objective is to identify commonalities among the input data samples. Reducing the dimensionality of a training dataset is another application of unsupervised machine learning, in which the most statistically relevant features are determined regardless of any labels.

Semi-Supervised Learning: focuses on implementing semi-supervised learning techniques directly on edge devices. Semi-supervised ML is defined as "machine learning that makes use of both labelled and unlabelled data during training." It is a hybrid of supervised and unsupervised machine learning [21]. Semi-supervised machine learning is helpful when labelling all samples in an extensive training dataset would be prohibitive from a time or cost perspective.

Self-Supervised Learning: focuses on implementing self-supervised learning techniques that generate implicit labels from unstructured data, rather than relying on labelled datasets for supervisory signals.

Reinforcement Learning: uses AI models to improve decision-making through trial-and-error. Reinforcement learning is the process of training an agent(s) to interact with its environment to achieve a predefined goal [21]. In reinforcement learning, a machine learning agent(s) learns through an iterative process of trial and error. The goal of agent(s) is to find the strategy (i.e. build a model) for obtaining the best rewards from the environment. For each trial (successful or not), the environment provides indirect feedback. Based on this feedback, the agent(s) then adjust their behaviour (i.e., their model) [21].

Federated Learning (FL): Federated learning is a decentralised machine learning approach in which multiple devices collaboratively train a model while each device sees only part of the data. Instead of sending data to a central server, each device trains the model locally using only its own data. The results are then sent to a central server, where they are aggregated to improve the global model. The rationales for federated learning often centre on privacy and/or certainty.

Transfer Learning: Refers to a series of methods where data intended for solving one problem is leveraged to apply the knowledge gained from it to a different problem [21]. For example, information gained from recognising house numbers in a street view can be used to recognise handwritten numbers.

Continuous Learning: Edge AI domain used for continuous AI model training. It is also known as continual learning or lifelong learning and is incremental training of a model that occurs continuously while the system is running in production. This is a particular case of retraining, where model updates are repeated, occur frequently, and do not interrupt operations [21]. In many AI systems, training occurs during development before deployment to production. This is like standard software development, where the system is built and tested fully before it is put into production. The behaviour of such systems is assessed during the verification process and is expected to remain unchanged during the operational phase. AI systems that embody continuous learning involve incremental updates to the model as it operates in production. The data input to the system during operation is analysed to produce an output and simultaneously used to adjust the model, improving it based on the production data. Continuous learning can help overcome the limitations of the original training data and address data and concept drift. However, it also presents significant challenges in ensuring that the AI system continues to operate correctly as it learns.

On-Device Training: Training a model directly on an edge device, like mobile phones, embedded systems, gaming consoles, web browsers, and more. This approach differs from training on a centralised server or in the cloud. On-device training is particularly valuable when data privacy is paramount and sharing it with external servers or clouds is not feasible. Additionally, it is advantageous for personalisation tasks, as the model can be tailored and trained directly on the user's device. Existing on-device training approaches and solutions cover: (i) last-layer or bias-only backpropagation; (ii) sparse backpropagation; (iii) complete backpropagation for fine-tuning; and (iv) complete backpropagation with optimised memory consumption.

Training Data: Consists of data samples used to train an ML algorithm. Typically, the data samples relate to a topic of concern and can consist of structured or unstructured data, both unlabelled and labelled. In the latter case, the label guides the machine learning model's training process [21].

Trained model: A trained model is the result of model training, which, in turn, is defined as the process of establishing or improving the parameters of a machine learning model using a machine learning algorithm and training data [21]. An ML model is a mathematical construct that generates an inference or prediction from input data. An AI system should use the trained model to make predictions based on production data from the area of interest. Various standardised formats exist for storing and transmitting the trained model as a set of numbers.

Generative AI (GenAI): AI that can create original content such as text, images, video, audio or software code in response to a prompt or request. GenAI uses advanced DL models, algorithms and transformers that simulate the learning and decision-making processes of the human brain. These models work by identifying and encoding patterns and relationships in large amounts of data, then using that information to understand users' natural language requests or questions and respond by creating new content based on learned patterns.

Diffusion Models: Generative models used primarily for image generation and other computer vision tasks. Diffusion-based neural networks are trained through deep learning to progressively "diffuse" samples with random noise, then reverse that diffusion process to generate high-quality images.

Variational Autoencoders (VAEs): Generative models used in ML to generate new data in the form of variations of the input data they're trained on. VAEs can perform tasks common to other autoencoders, such as denoising.

Transformers: Neural network architectures that transform or change an input sequence into an output sequence. The transformer models are trained on sequential data to generate extended sequences of content, such as shapes in an image, words in a sentence, frames of a video, commands in software code, etc. The transformer model uses an internal mathematical representation to identify the relevance and relationships between the content, and it uses that knowledge to generate the output.

Multimodal AI: Refers to machine learning models capable of processing and integrating information from multiple modalities or types of data. These modalities can include text, images, audio, video and other forms of sensory input. Multimodal AI combines and analyses different forms of data inputs to achieve a more comprehensive understanding and generate more robust outputs.

Retrieval Augmented Generation (RAG): Architecture for optimising the performance of an AI model by connecting it with external knowledge bases and supporting LLMs and SLMs in generating more relevant responses of higher quality. RAG enhances AI applications by retrieving relevant information from databases, documents, or the web and supplying it as real-time context to LLMs, improving accuracy and relevance without requiring retraining.

Generative Adversarial Network (GAN): ML model designed to generate realistic data by learning patterns from existing training datasets. It operates within an unsupervised learning framework using DL techniques, where two neural networks work in opposition: one generates data, and the other evaluates whether it is real or generated.

Large Language Models (LLMs): A category of deep learning models trained on very large amounts of data, making them capable of understanding and generating natural language and other types of content to perform a wide range of tasks by including processing and analysing long text sequences. LLMs are built on neural network architectures such as transformers, which excel at handling sequences of words and capturing patterns in text. LLMs can understand context, generate human-like text, translate languages, and even write various types of creative content.

Small Language Models (SLMs): Smaller AI models capable of processing, understanding and generating natural language content and can be deployed at the edge. SLM parameters, which are internal variables, such as weights and biases, that the model learns during training, range from a few million to a few billion.

Vision Language Models (VLMs): VLMs are AI models that combine and mix computer vision and NLP capabilities and learn to map the relationships between text data and visual data, such as images or videos and generate text from visual inputs or understand natural language prompts in the context of visual information. The VLMs combine LLMs and SLMs with vision models or ML algorithms. VLMs are multimodal AI systems that use text and images or videos as input and produce text as output, in the form of image or video descriptions, answering questions about an image or identifying parts of an image or objects in a video.

Agentic AI: Refers to the broader class of AI and edge systems designed with intrinsic agency that can accomplish a specific goal with limited supervision. Agentic AI possesses the capacity to initiate actions, maintain persistent memory of its state, and pursue abstract goals over extended horizons. It consists of AI agents, ML models that mimic human decision-making to solve problems in real time. In a MAS, each agent performs a specific subtask required to reach the goal and their efforts are coordinated through AI orchestration. Agentic architecture supports and regulates the behaviour of AI-powered agents operating within a GenAI system. Agentic AI systems require their agents to be adaptive and navigate dynamic environments to achieve desired outcomes. Agentic AI exhibits autonomy, goal-driven behaviour and adaptability. The term "agentic" refers to these models' agency, or the capacity to act independently and goal-oriented by using generated content from LLMs, SLMs, and VLMs to complete complex tasks autonomously by calling external tools. The functions used in implementing agentic AI systems are perception and input handling, planning and task decomposition, reasoning and decision-making, action and tool calling, communication, learning and adaptation and memory.

AI Agents: The discrete software implementations of agentic AI. Agents are characterised by their autonomy loop: perceive, reason, decide, act and memorise. is a system that autonomously performs tasks by designing workflows with available tools and can encompass a wide range of functions beyond natural language processing, including decision-making, problem-solving, interacting with external environments and performing actions. AI agents solve complex tasks across applications, including software design, IT automation, code generation and conversational assistance. AI agents use advanced natural language processing techniques of LLMs, SLMs, and VLMs to comprehend and respond to user inputs step-by-step and determine when to call on external tools. AI agents are classified based on their level of intelligence, decision-making processes, and how they interact with their surroundings to achieve desired outcomes, in categories such as simple reflex agents, model-based reflex agents, goal-based agents, utility-based agents, and learning agents. Some agents operate purely on predefined rules, while others use learning algorithms to refine their behaviour.

Multi-Agent Systems (MAS): MAS consists of multiple artificial intelligence (AI) agents working collectively to perform tasks on behalf of a user or another system. Each agent in a MAS has individual properties, but all agents collaborate to achieve desired global properties. Multi-agent systems are effective at completing large-scale, complex tasks that involve many agents.

Multi-Agentic AI: Involves the interaction of multiple autonomous agents sharing a common environment. This field studies the dynamics of cooperation, competition, and coordination. On the road, traffic is inherently a multi-agent system where every vehicle, pedestrian, and cyclist is an independent agent with its own objectives. Multi-Agentic AI models aim to predict the collective behaviour of these entities to enable safe and efficient navigation, moving beyond simple obstacle avoidance to sophisticated social negotiation.

Agentic RAG: Defined as the use of AI agents to support RAG. Agentic RAG systems add AI agents to the RAG pipeline to increase adaptability and accuracy, enabling LLMs and SLMs to retrieve information from multiple sources and handle extended, complex workflows.

Distributed Intelligence: Refers to systems where multiple agents or entities collaborate and share information to achieve a common goal or solve complex problems. It leverages the collective capabilities of these agents, for example, through distributed computing, to enhance overall performance, adaptability, and scalability. The concept is often applied in Multi-Agent Systems (MAS), enabling them to learn from each other's experiences and improve their collective perception and decision-making. It allows for more adaptive, scalable, and complex problem-solving with minimal human intervention.

First Principles: Edge AI domain that arises from the fundamental properties and behaviours of persisting physical systems, such as energy, entropy, and the ability to maintain and propagate information over time. By deducing intelligence from these first principles, we understand it as the optimisation of actions and decisions that align with the natural laws governing the system's environment and as an emergent capacity of a system to process information, adapt, and achieve goals within the constraints of a physical universe [77].

Computer Vision: Edge AI domain that processes visual information from cameras, sensors, or is stored on a device at the edge, enabling applications like facial recognition, object detection, and video analytics.

Machine Vision: A branch of engineering that designs and implements systems that allow machines to interpret visual information locally on the device. Machine Vision systems include optical sensors, hardware, algorithms, data storage and processing. Enables instant analysis and action based on visual input, which is essential for applications such as autonomous vehicles, manufacturing quality inspection, and live security monitoring.

Speech Systems: Edge AI domain that addresses the deployment of speech recognition, processing, and generation technologies using AI directly on edge audio devices. The approach facilitates real-time processing and analysis of audio data at the point of capture, leveraging the benefits of edge computing.

Predictive Analytics: Edge AI domain that utilises historical data to forecast future outcomes and provide predictive maintenance and anomaly detection.

Robotics and Control Systems: Edge AI domain that implements real-time AI-driven decision-making for robotic movements and industrial automation.

Planning Optimisation and Scheduling Systems: An edge AI domain that focuses on deploying sophisticated algorithms to manage and optimise tasks, resources, and processes in real-time directly on edge devices. These systems aim to enhance operational efficiency, improve decision-making, and enable autonomous functionality across settings from industrial automation to smart home management.

2.3 Edge AI System Elements

The development of edge AI solutions leads to the emergence of multimodal edge AI implementations that yield real-time performance at the edge for various industrial sectors. These require the integration of edge AI hardware, software, AI technology stack building blocks and data in an edge AI design framework for the whole system, as illustrated in Figure 2.3.

Defining the non-functional and functional requirements, aligned with quality properties, supports to address holistically all the edge AI system components including hardware, software, AI techniques/methods and data and treat edge AI systems as a set of systems and system elements that interact to provide a unique intelligent capabilities that none of the constituent systems can accomplish on its own facilitating interaction of the constituent systems in this system of systems concept.

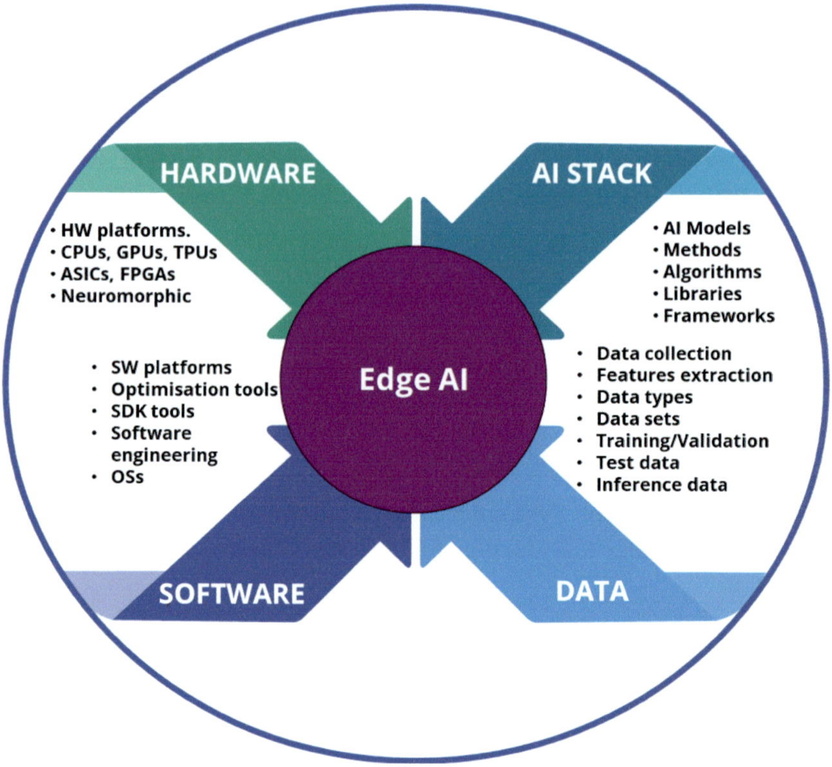

Figure 2.3 Edge AI system components.

Developing a conceptual framework for edge AI system of systems design and implementation is critical to be used as a reference for defining the functional and non-functional requirements of edge AI systems across the computing continuum and various industrial applications.

2.3.1 Edge AI Technology Stack

Edge AI technology encompasses a multi-layered approach that facilitates the deployment of AI capabilities directly at the edge. This architecture allows for efficient data processing, analysis, and decision-making closer to where data is generated, significantly reducing latency and bandwidth usage. A five-layer edge AI technology stack is presented in Figure 2.4 [69].

Edge AI hardware is the foundational layer, which contains at least three components reflecting the processing units responsible for performing

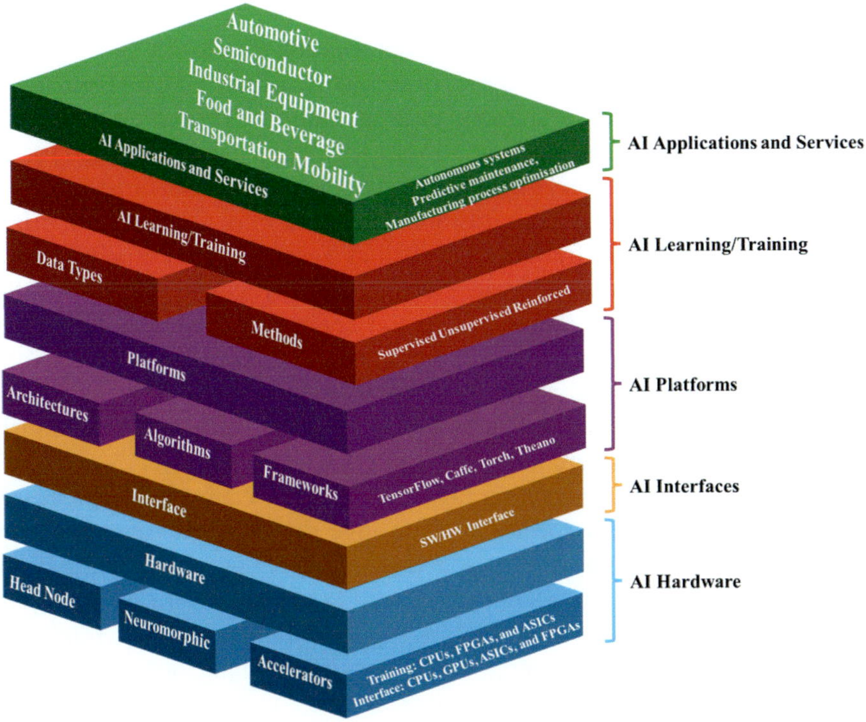

Figure 2.4 Edge AI technology stack layers [69].

specialised AI operations. The neuromorphic hardware components consist of new ultra-low-power silicon chip architectures (e.g., neuromorphic modules and chips, digital, analogue, spike NN) incorporating different chip designs and algorithms to mimic how the human brain works. The accelerator set of components consists of silicon chips designed to perform highly parallel functions and accelerate AI workloads required during training and inference, such as GPUs, NPUs, VPUs, TPUs, FPGAs, or ASICs. The HW layer includes in-memory computing architectures to support high-speed data processing within the chip, essential for handling real-time AI applications. Energy efficiency is critical for HW designs that enable AI calculations on remote edge devices without excessive energy consumption.

Edge AI interfaces layer covers the mechanisms through which edge devices communicate with each other and with other parts of the system, ensuring seamless data exchange and control. The head node components coordinate computations among accelerators and provides interfaces for developers to integrate AI functionalities into devices and applications. Interfaces can include technology for preprocessing data locally.

Edge AI platforms provide the infrastructure for deploying and managing AI models on edge devices, incorporating tools for model development, optimisation, deployment, and monitoring. The platforms layer is used for AI and ML/DL deployment and consists of three sublayers, which aim to abstract firmware from the underlying hardware. The framework sublayer comprises packages that trigger AI frameworks, such as TensorFlow, TensorFlow Lite, Caffe, PyTorch, Theano, etc., via the interface layer, which connects the hardware and platform layers and facilitates communication. The algorithms sublayer consists of rules to achieve optimal inference according to the training method employed, such as backpropagation, evolutionary, and contrasted divergence. The architectures sublayer consists of many continuously evolving neural network architectures, such as CNN, RNN, etc.

The edge AI learning/training layer involves the methods and processes used to train AI models specifically for edge device deployment, emphasising the need for lightweight, adaptable models. The layer consists of two sublayers. The methods sublayer involves techniques for optimising the model for specific domain data, such as supervised, unsupervised, reinforcement, and first-principles learning. Techniques like pruning, quantisation, and knowledge distillation aimed at reducing model complexity and size while maintaining accuracy are part of this sublayer. Different learning approaches, such as federated learning, are included, where models are trained across numerous decentralised devices without sharing raw data, enhancing privacy and reducing the need for data transfer. The data type sublayer consists of categories of domain input data, such as labelled and unlabelled data.

The edge AI applications and services layer consists of end-user applications and services that leverage AI at the edge to deliver value and insights. Solutions can be customised based on generic data or customer-specific training data. The AI technology stack provides a common understanding of the AI layers and components when implementing and benchmarking various AI technologies and applications.

By integrating these layers, edge AI technology delivers intelligent solutions directly at the data generation and use site. This layered approach facilitates the development of edge AI applications tailored for specific tasks and the enhancement of existing systems with real-time learning, adaptability, and efficiency.

2.3.2 Hardware

Edge AI hardware refers to the computing devices designed to perform AI computations directly at the edge of networks, near the source of data generation across the micro-, deep- and meta-edge continuum. The primary goal of edge AI hardware is to enable real-time data processing, reduce latency, and enhance privacy by optimising and reducing data transmission.

Edge AI systems can run on various hardware platforms and take different forms, from central processing units (CPUs), and microcontroller units (MCUs) to advanced neural processing units (NPUs). The edge AI hardware is designed as compact system on a chip (SoC), system on modules (SoMs), and Application-Specific Integrated Circuits (ASICs) that consume minimal power, making it suitable for deployment in mobile, portable, or remote edge devices.

An ASIC is an integrated circuit customised for a particular use. ASICs are an option for providing AI-specific functionality. An ASIC can be customised as an accelerator to speed up the AI process by offering functions such as dedicated parallel multiplying-accumulating blocks, optimised memory allocation and lower precision arithmetic. ASICs provide a higher computational capability for AI with lower spatial volumes, cost and energy consumption. ASICs enable AI to be implemented in space- and power-constrained edge IoT devices [21].

An SoC is an integrated circuit integrating on a single substrate/chip or microchip multiple cores, including a mix of CPUs, GPUs, TPUs, and other types of functional units, e.g., digital signal processors (DSPs), neural processing units (NPUs), image signal processors, (ISPs), memory, input/output ports, secondary storage, and sometimes Wi-Fi and cellular modems. SoC organisation enhances performance and reduces energy consumption and semiconductor die area compared with motherboard-based architecture with equivalent functionality but discrete components.

A SoM is a board-level circuit that integrates an embedded processing system function in a single module that includes microprocessor cores, SoCs, memory blocks, communication interfaces, and hardware peripherals on a single production-ready substrate. SoMs offer a flexible and modular approach to system design.

The edge AI HW includes specialised processing units, such as AI accelerators implemented as GPUs (Graphics Processing Units), TPUs (Tensor Processing Units), NPUs, Vision Processing Units (VPUs) and neuromorphic units, that are optimised for the parallel processing requirements of AI workloads. Field-Programmable Gate Arrays (FPGAs) and ASICs are also used to deliver high efficiency for specific AI tasks, providing customisable solutions tailored to various applications.

Increased performance edge AI HW is necessary to deal with the aggregation of multiple endpoints, multimodality of data and cross-inference from many sources. This increased functionality and breadth of scope also increases the consequence of faults, so the requirements for security and reliable operation also increase as one moves away from the micro-edge. New edge processing circuits and devices with novel processing architectures are emerging for edge AI implementations, including integrating several accelerators and processing units (CPUs, GPUs, TPUs, NPUs, ISPs, VPUs) into one chip or SoM circuit.

Edge AI implementations require low-power AI accelerator architectures (e.g., VPU, GPU, TPU) suitable for edge devices and the given application use case. They must also establish an appropriate deployment platform, learning frameworks (e.g., TensorFlow, PyTorch, TensorFlow Lite, ONNXruntime, TensorRT) that meets the required needs and a robust programming language (Python, C++) suitable for edge AI development and the platform/framework.

Edge AI hardware is equipped with the necessary computational power to run inference tasks locally, allowing devices to make predictions and decisions in real-time based on new data inputs. The HW supports various connectivity options, such as Wi-Fi, Bluetooth, and cellular networks, to communicate efficiently with other devices and systems. Deep- and meta-edge AI hardware can have the necessary computational power to partially and fully train AI models.

The HW provides the computational power necessary for real-time data analysis and decision-making based on AI algorithms and is optimised to reduce latency and increase bandwidth efficiency, which is critical for real-time applications. The HW facilitates easier scaling of AI applications, as deploying additional edge devices can enhance overall processing without overwhelming centralised resources.

As computing performance increases, edge AI hardware is advancing to enable the local processing of more complex AI models and larger datasets. This is driven by chip design and architecture innovations that optimise performance and energy consumption.

2.3.3 Software

Edge AI software and platforms provide the tools and frameworks to develop, deploy, and manage AI models directly on edge devices. These solutions effectively harness edge hardware's computational power, offering flexibility and efficiency in implementing AI applications across various environments.

Edge AI software platforms often include tools for model optimisation, such as pruning, quantisation, and knowledge distillation. These techniques reduce the size of AI models and improve their performance on resource-constrained devices without significantly compromising accuracy.

Edge AI software supports AI frameworks like TensorFlow, PyTorch, Keras, ONNX, and Caffe, enabling developers to use familiar tools and libraries while ensuring models can be executed efficiently on edge devices.

Software Development Kits (SDKs) and Application Programming Interfaces (APIs) are tailored for edge environments, simplifying integrating AI capabilities into applications.

Edge AI software can be categorised into various types based on functionality and use cases. Some common categories of edge AI software include:

- **Machine and Deep Learning Frameworks:** These libraries and tools allow developers to build, train, and deploy machine learning models.
- **Natural Language Processing (NLP) Software:** NLP software enables machines to understand, interpret, and generate human language.
- **Computer and Machine Vision Software:** These tools focus on image and video analysis, enabling AI systems to understand and interpret visual data.
- **Speech Recognition and Synthesis Software:** This category includes software that can transcribe spoken language into text and generate speech from written text.
- **Edge AI Chatbots and Virtual Assistants:** These applications use natural language processing and machine learning to interact with users and provide relevant information or services.
- **Reinforcement Learning Frameworks:** These tools are designed to develop edge AI systems that learn through trial and error, often used in robotics and autonomous applications.
- **Active inference frameworks:** These tools allow to formulate agents with adaptive behaviour to the deployment scenario, which inherits from

the physics of self-organization, i.e., first-principles. These tools enable maximizing (Bayesian) model evidence, via inference, learning, and model selection. Edge AI Development Platforms: These platforms offer end-to-end solutions for building, training, and deploying AI models, often with pre-built models and drag-and-drop interfaces.

- **Edge AI Data Annotation Tools:** These tools help label and annotate data to train edge AI models.
- **Edge AI-based Business Solutions:** These are edge AI applications designed to solve specific business problems.

Edge AI platforms often support deployment across heterogeneous devices, ensuring that AI models work cohesively within diverse hardware ecosystems.

Edge AI software and platforms support edge AI system developers in creating robust, scalable, and efficient AI solutions that leverage the full potential of edge computing. By focusing on optimisation, compatibility, and ease of deployment, these tools make it possible to meet the varied demands of real-world applications that require speed, reliability, and autonomy.

Example of edge AI software platforms:

ST Edge AI Suite: This suite offers a set of tools and software solutions to simplify the development and deployment of AI applications on edge devices, particularly those powered by STM's microcontrollers and microprocessors. The suite caters to developers looking to implement AI capabilities such as machine learning and neural network inference directly on low-power, resource-constrained devices.

eIQ® Auto Machine Learning (ML) Toolkit: Offers a suite of tools aimed at simplifying and accelerating the deployment of machine learning models on edge devices, particularly within the automotive sector. This toolkit is part of NXP's broader eIQ Machine Learning Software Development Environment, designed to cater to various ML applications across diverse hardware platforms offered by NXP.

Google Coral: Provides the Edge TPU with an SDK for accelerating ML inferencing at the edge, supporting TensorFlow Lite models.

NVIDIA Jetson: Offers a comprehensive platform with SDKs like JetPack and deep learning tools that support high-performance AI applications.

Azure IoT Edge: Microsoft's platform for deploying AI workloads on the edge, integrated with Azure cloud services for a seamless hybrid solution.

AWS Greengrass: Facilitates the execution of local computing, messaging, and machine learning inference capabilities on connected devices.

OpenVINO Toolkit: Developed by Intel, optimises AI model performance on Intel hardware across CPUs, VPUs, FPGAs, and integrated GPUs.

2.3.4 Edge AI Frameworks, Methods, and Techniques

Edge AI frameworks are software libraries and tools designed to simplify and facilitate the deployment, development, and optimisation of edge AI models on edge devices. These frameworks address the unique challenges and requirements of edge computing, where resources such as processing power, memory, and energy are often constrained.

Edge AI frameworks enable the deployment of pre-trained AI models on various edge devices, ensuring they perform efficiently in resource-constrained environments by using techniques like quantisation, pruning, and sparsification to reduce the size and computational requirements of AI models, making them suitable for edge conditions. This ensures compatibility with machine learning libraries and frameworks like TensorFlow, PyTorch, and ONNX, allowing developers to leverage existing models and facilitate efficient data preprocessing and handling on edge devices to support real-time analytics and decision-making.

The edge AI frameworks support multiple AI models, including deep learning neural networks, machine learning algorithms, and computer vision models. They are designed with a small footprint to operate effectively on devices with limited resources without compromising performance.

TensorFlow Lite: An extension of TensorFlow designed to run machine learning models on mobile and edge devices. It supports model optimisation through quantisation and provides an interpreter capable of running efficiently on various types of hardware accelerators.

ONNX Runtime: An open-source inference engine focused on providing performance-enhanced runtime options for models expressed in the ONNX format. It provides extensive hardware compatibility, supporting CPU, GPU, and custom accelerators.

Apache MXNet: A flexible and efficient deep learning framework supported by open-source. With its Gluon API, MXNet is efficient for training and deploying models on edge devices in real time.

NVIDIA TensorRT: A high-performance deep learning inference library specifically for NVIDIA GPUs and designed to accelerate inference for deep learning models.

OpenVINO Toolkit: Developed by Intel, it optimises and deploys AI inference across Intel architectures, including CPUs, integrated GPUs, and FPGAs, primarily for vision applications.

Arm NN: Provides an inference engine optimised for Arm Cortex CPUs and GPUs, enabling efficient execution of neural networks on edge devices.

2.3.5 Data

Data plays a multifaceted role in edge AI systems, serving as the foundation upon which these systems operate and derive insights. The characteristics and handling of data significantly influence the performance, reliability, and efficiency of edge AI applications.

Several challenges relate to data in edge AI, among them data quality, volume, and integration. Data quality ensures that the data used for training and inference is accurate and representative of real-world conditions, which is vital for model reliability. Data volume requires handling volumes of data generated by numerous devices to match edge devices' processing power and storage capacity. Integrating data from diverse sources and formats is complex in heterogeneous environments with different types of devices and sensors requiring new multi-modality techniques and algorithms.

Data is driving the ability of edge AI systems to learn, adapt, and make informed decisions quickly and efficiently. As edge AI continues to evolve, strategies to optimise data usage focus on quality, security, and efficient processing.

The datasets used in edge AI applications span various domains and can differ based on the application and field for which the edge AI model is being developed. Several categories of edge AI datasets based on their applications are presented below:

Anomaly Detection Datasets are designed to train edge AI models to identify anomalies or outliers in various types of data, such as electrical signals, network traffic, industrial machinery, motors, or the behaviour of edge devices.

Audio and Speech Datasets encompass audio recordings paired with corresponding transcriptions or labels. These datasets are essential for developing edge AI models for speech recognition, keyword spotting, speaker identification, and other audio-related tasks.

Environmental Datasets consist of data collected from sensors that monitor environmental parameters such as temperature, humidity, and air quality. These datasets are utilised for applications in environmental monitoring and sustainability.

Gesture and Motion Datasets involve data captured from sensors like accelerometers and gyroscopes to recognise human gestures or movements. These datasets are used in gesture and human activity recognition applications.

Healthcare Datasets focus on applications related to healthcare, including medical image analysis, disease diagnosis, and patient monitoring.

Image Classification Datasets consist of images labelled with corresponding class identifiers. These datasets are used to train and evaluate edge AI models for tasks such as object recognition and scene classification.

Natural Language Processing (NLP) Datasets for edge AI models contain text data and corresponding labels or annotations. These datasets are applied in text classification, sentiment analysis, and named entity recognition tasks.

Object Detection Datasets feature images annotated with bounding boxes around objects of interest. These datasets are essential for training edge AI models to detect and localise one or multiple objects within an image. Object detection is a critical technique in computer vision that involves identifying relevant objects in images and video frames. The algorithms used for object detection employ advanced machine learning and deep learning architectures to analyse image data and recognise and pinpoint objects of interest. The output typically includes the object's name and a bounding box indicating its location. Deep learning architectures for object detection include Single Shot Detector (SSD), You Only Look Once (YOLO), and Region-based Convolutional Neural Networks (R-CNN), among others.

Semantic Segmentation Datasets provide pixel-level annotations for each image, indicating the class to which each pixel belongs. These datasets are utilised for tasks like image segmentation and instance segmentation.

Time Series Datasets are employed across edge AI applications, including IoT sensor data, equipment health monitoring, predictive maintenance, and forecasting. These datasets contain sequential data points, including timestamps and associated target values.

3

Edge AI System Engineering

Edge AI system engineering is a holistic and interdisciplinary approach to designing, developing, and managing edge AI systems. It involves applying principles, methods, and tools to define, analyse, and validate system requirements and specifications.

3.1 Systems Engineering

Systems engineering is a systematic, interdisciplinary approach to a system's design, implementation, technical management, operation, and eventual retirement. A "system" is an integrated assembly of elements that collectively deliver the capability necessary to fulfil a specific need. These elements encompass all hardware, software, equipment, facilities, personnel, processes, and procedures required to achieve the desired system-level outcomes. The outcomes include system-level qualities, properties, characteristics, functions, behaviours, and performance metrics. The unique value of the system, beyond the sum of its parts and components, is primarily derived from the interrelationships and interactions among these parts, emphasising the importance of their integration. This holistic perspective is crucial when making technical decisions, ensuring that stakeholder requirements for functional, physical, and operational performance are met within the intended use environment throughout the system's lifecycle, all while adhering to constraints related to cost, schedule, and other factors. Systems engineering thus serves as a disciplined methodology that helps manage and contain the life cycle costs of a system, embodying a logical and structured way of thinking.

Systems engineering focuses on developing an operable system that meets specified requirements within often conflicting constraints. It is a holistic, integrative discipline where the contributions of various engineering specialities, such as electrical engineering, software engineering, power engineering, and human factors engineering, are evaluated and balanced against one another to create a cohesive whole. This approach ensures that no single discipline's perspective dominates the system design.

DOI: 10.1201/9788743809586-3

The system's engineering aims to achieve a safe and balanced design amidst competing interests and multiple, sometimes conflicting constraints. Throughout the process, continuous validation is essential to confirm that the system's operational goals are being met. This balanced and integrative approach ensures that the final system is robust, efficient, and capable of fulfilling its intended purpose.

A foundational principle of systems engineering is its lifecycle perspective as the development is viewed as a comprehensive process that encompasses concept development, engineering development, upgradability and post-development stages, including production, operations, training, support, and eventual disposal. By considering the entire lifecycle, systems engineering helps to mitigate risks and ensure the long-term viability and success of the system.

Traditional systems engineering lifecycle models, such as the sequential waterfall method or the more structured V-model, are predicated on a development process that flows from well-defined requirements to design, implementation, and validation. These models are applied in domains where the problem is well understood, and system behaviour is deterministic. Still, they are not well-suited for the development of edge AI systems, which are characterised by non-determinism, probabilistic reasoning, and emergent behaviours [22]. The edge AI model's performance is not guaranteed by its code but is a learned property derived from data, making its behaviour inherently uncertain.

As a result, the edge AI development lifecycle must be iterative, data-centric, and adaptive. The process is not a linear progression but a continuous cycle of data collection, model development, model training and re-training, testing, and deployment, where feedback from each stage interacts with the following. This development requires a co-design approach where the edge AI models, the target hardware, the system software, the data and data sets are not developed in sequence but are considered and optimised in parallel. This holistic perspective is captured by the data-model-HW/SW system optimisation quadruple, which asserts that these four interconnected elements must be engineered in concert to achieve a viable solution. The choice of a hardware accelerator (system) influences the type of software (system), which will determine which model architectures can be run efficiently (model), which in turn dictates the nature and volume of data required for training (data) [23].

The edge AI development lifecycle is iterative, exploratory and emergent. The system's final capabilities and performance characteristics are often discovered through empirical experimentation rather than being fully specified at the outset. A traditional iterative model assumes that while the system is constructed in increments, the overarching requirements are known and stable. In many AI-driven systems, the requirements themselves can be ambiguous (e.g., "accurately detect a threat"), and their feasibility is unknown until a model is trained and evaluated on representative real-world data [24].

The development workflow in edge AI systems can be represented by a series of experiments designed to answer questions about feasibility and performance. Each cycle or iteration of data collection, training, and testing is an experiment to determine whether a specific level of performance, such as a target accuracy, is achievable within the given resource constraints. In this development workflow, it is vital to consider the concept drift, where the statistical properties of the operational environment change over time, degrading model performance and necessitating a continuous lifecycle of monitoring, re-evaluation, and re-training to maintain the edge AI system's suitability.

The complexity and unique constraints of edge AI systems demand the rigorous application of core systems engineering principles. These principles provide the structure and discipline necessary to manage development, mitigate risks, and ensure the final system is robust, reliable, and fit for purpose. Principles such as modularity, decomposition, systematic trade-off analysis, and verification and validation can be applied to edge AI requirements.

Modularity is the practice of decomposing a complex system into smaller, independent, and interchangeable components or modules to meet the requirements of these components. In edge AI system design, this principle is critical for managing the inherent complexity. A monolithic design is challenging to develop, test, and maintain. By breaking the system into logical modules, such as a data acquisition module, a data pre-processing module, an inference engine, and a decision logic module, the requirements can be applied in parallel, and the system becomes more scalable and maintainable. This approach applies to both software, to structure the AI workflow, and hardware, where modular components enable flexible and resilient system configurations [29].

Trade-off analysis is essential for edge AI systems engineering. The constrained nature of edge devices imposes the need to make decisions that balance conflicting requirements. There is a continuous challenge between competing quality attributes: improving model accuracy often increases computational complexity, which in turn increases inference latency and power consumption [30]. Enhancing security through encryption may add computational overhead, again impacting performance. These are not choices that can be made informally; they require a systematic and evidence-based process. Formal methodologies, such as the weighted sum method or multi-attribute utility theory, provide structured frameworks for evaluating alternatives against a set of weighted criteria, enabling engineers to make proper decisions that align with project priorities [31]

Verification and validation (V&V) in the context of edge AI presents challenges that are different from those of traditional software testing. For conventional systems, V&V is the process of confirming that the system was built correctly according to its specifications. For edge AI-based systems, this is complicated by their non-deterministic nature and because the system's behaviour is probabilistic. AI models can be vulnerable to adversarial examples based on subtly perturbed inputs designed to cause misclassification, which exposes a unique failure mode that must be tested. The V&V process for edge AI must therefore encompass comprehensive data validation to check for quality and bias, rigorous model validation to assess performance on unseen data, and robustness testing to evaluate the system's resilience to adversarial attacks and unexpected environmental conditions.

In edge AI engineering, trade-off analysis and V&V are not discrete, sequential phases but are instead two components of a single, continuous feedback loop that drives the iterative lifecycle. While traditional engineering may conduct a trade study early in the design phase to select an architecture, in edge AI, the core trade-offs are influenced at every stage. The application of model compression techniques like quantisation or pruning is a direct implementation of the accuracy-versus-latency trade-off. The V&V process does not produce a simple pass/fail result but rather a set of statistical performance measures, such as "the AI model is 98% accurate and consumes 10 mW". This output is quantitative data that serves as the direct input for the next stage of trade-off analysis, prompting the designer to determine whether the performance change is an acceptable price for the resource savings. V&V is thus transformed from a quality assurance element into an ongoing system characterisation process that fuels continuous, informed decision-making.

3.2 Requirements Engineering

Requirement engineering (RE) is the process of formalising and defining needs at each stage of system design, including customer requirements, design requirements, and testing requirements. It focuses on identifying, tracing, and characterising these needs to ensure their implementation and impact are clearly understood and deals with developing and verifying the system requirements.

RE is an addition to systems engineering and focuses on an essential concept in implementing systems engineering: practices related to the process (e.g., quality, standards to be applied) or product development (e.g., non-functional, functional requirements).

RE is the discipline of establishing user requirements and specifying hardware, software, AI, and data systems. Defining requirements involves determining what users want from a system and understanding what the needs mean regarding design. It is closely related to hardware, software, AI, and data engineering and focuses on designing and developing the system that users want.

Following good requirements engineering practices helps achieve the primary objective of ensuring that the delivered system meets the customer's needs. Requirements engineering consists of establishing and documenting requirements. The various activities associated with requirements engineering are formulation, elicitation, specification, analysis, verification and validation, and management. Requirements formulation involves collecting, organising, communicating, and managing requirements. Recommended practices for software requirements specifications are provided in [54].

Several standards focus on requirements engineering. One example is ISO/IEC/ IEEE 29148-2018 [55], which addresses requirements engineering and specifies the required processes implemented in the engineering activities that result in requirements for systems and software products (including services) throughout the life cycle.

For edge AI systems, a disciplined, requirements-driven approach is essential, but its application demands a considerable paradigm shift away from traditional practices. The fundamental challenge lies in transitioning from a specification-driven development model, where system behaviour is explicitly defined, to a data-driven one, where system capabilities are learned and requirements are often emergent, probabilistic, and difficult to articulate with deterministic certainty [24].

This shift necessitates the introduction of new categories of requirements that are paramount in AI systems. While traditional RE focuses heavily on functional requirements, edge AI engineering must elevate the importance of data requirements, which concern the quality, quantity, format, and representativeness of the data used for training and testing the model [24]. Equally critical are model requirements, which define the desired qualitative attributes of the AI model itself, such as its explainability, transparency, and fairness. Finally, the autonomous nature of these systems brings ethical requirements to the forefront, demanding that the system be lawful, prevent harm, and respect human values [24].

The RE process itself must also adapt. Elicitation can no longer rely solely on stakeholder interviews; it must incorporate data-centric activities and may be augmented by AI-powered tools that can analyse large volumes of text or user feedback to identify latent needs [25]. The act of specifying requirements also changes. The precision and iterative refinement involved in prompt engineering for large language models offer a useful analogy for how requirements for AI systems must be crafted: with clarity, context, and a willingness to refine based on the system's response.

This evolution changes the very definition of a requirement in the context of systems engineering. A requirement for an edge AI system evolves from being a static, deterministic statement of need into a dynamic, negotiated contract of acceptable performance under conditions of uncertainty.

For a task like "recognise a stop sign," a complete, deterministic specification that covers every possible real-world variation is impossible. Therefore, the requirement cannot be "The system shall correctly identify all stop signs." Instead, the requirement specification must define the acceptable bounds of the system's probabilistic behaviour. It becomes a composite statement comprising three key elements: (1) a set of evaluation measures, such as recall and precision; (2) criteria for acceptable values of these measures, such as "recall shall be greater than 99.5% and precision shall be greater than 98%"; and (3) a description of the operational context and data used to validate these criteria [26, 27]. This transforms the requirement into a testable element that explicitly captures the agreed-upon trade-offs, for example: "The system shall achieve a minimum F1-score of 0.9 for object detection while maintaining an end-to-end latency below 33 ms and consuming less than 200 mW of power."

Distributed AI-intensive systems raise several challenges for requirements and systems engineering. To guarantee a desired AI system behaviour, it is essential to ensure system attributes such as safety, robustness, and quality, and to establish process support, which involves addressing four key areas [28]:

- Defining contextual descriptions and requirements by properly describing and formulating requirements on the context in which an AI-intensive system is operated. For example, if a trained machine learning model is placed in another context, desired system behaviour and especially safety attributes can no longer be guaranteed without retraining the model on the new context.
- Setting data attributes and requirements considering the need for proper definitions of quality attributes of, and requirements on data that are used in the AI-intensive system. It is argued that data is the most critical element of an AI system and that system quality attributes, such as safety and robustness, cannot be provided without the ability to ensure such properties on the data used in the system.
- Establishing performance definitions in the context and data of an AI-intensive system raises the question of how the fulfilment of these requirements and the performance of the AI-intensive system can be monitored, considering that it is vital to understand first what needs to be monitored, before asking how it can be measured and monitored.
- Considering human factors and how to integrate human factor requirements in the AI-based system development process to increase the safety, acceptance and trust.

It is important to prioritise RE in the lifecycle development of AI and edge AI before the technical implementation, which extends to explainability (XAI) and its holistic incorporation as well. Explainability is an emerging non-functional requirement that has been highlighted as a critical quality aspect. When developing and deploying AI technologies, RE is essential to understand and document the needs, expectations, and constraints of different stakeholders. To ensure transparency, interpretability, and accountability of the AI system, it is crucial to involve end-users, domain experts, regulatory bodies, and ethicists in identifying and articulating the requirements related to explainability [32].

Requirements engineering principles can support the definition of FRs and NFRs, which serve different, unique purposes. FRs outline the provided functionality by the system, focusing on user needs and specific tasks [35] and are defined in such a way that they are testable with input-output pairs, even though this is not always feasible. NFRs do not detail what the system does, but rather how it does it, i.e., they highlight quality attributes and user experience, often requiring qualitative evaluations due to the difficulty of measuring or testing them directly [34]. FRs shape the system's core functionalities, whereas NFRs specify quality goals [33].

An overview of the landscape of techniques and practices in RE for ML is provided in [36].

As generative AI models evolve, they will be utilised in systems and requirements engineering to improve the analysis and classification of engineering requirements for edge AI systems, which underpin product design and development in these areas.

Classifying requirements in software systems is an established practice that involves addressing specific, categorised tasks in software or quality requirements, for standardised classification as defined by INCOSE's (International Council on Systems Engineering) standards [37] using categories such as FRs and NFRs. The advancements in generative AI can offer rapid and accurate analyses that increase systems engineers' efficiency. Challenges remain due to AI's disposition to generate misinterpretations, as seen in diverse applications [38, 39].

The study presented in [40] explores how generative AI can help automate and improve key steps in systems engineering. It examines AI's ability to analyse system requirements based on INCOSE's good requirement criteria, identifying well-formed and poorly written requirements. The AI models used classify requirements and explain why some do not meet the standards. The study evaluates the accuracy and reliability of AI in identifying quality issues by comparing AI assessments with those of experienced human engineers and explores AI's ability to classify FRs and NFRs and generate test specifications based on these classifications. The study aims to assess AI's potential to streamline engineering processes and improve learning outcomes through both quantitative and qualitative analysis, highlighting the challenges and limitations of AI, ensuring its safe and ethical use in professional and academic settings [40].

3.2.1 Requirements Engineering Evolution

The process of defining requirements is evolving as edge AI systems incorporate autonomous functions and new technologies to address what users want from the system and require understanding the implications for the design of these systems.

One of the primary objectives of edge AI system architecture is to determine the optimal partitioning of the system. This process involves

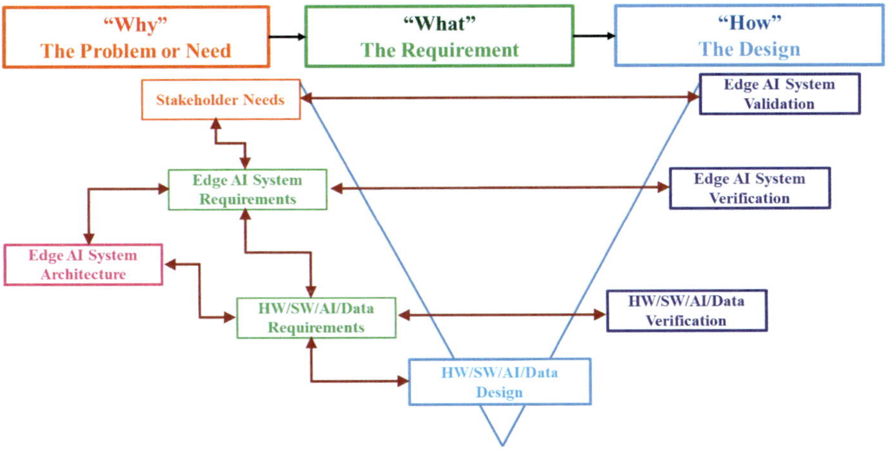

Figure 3.1 The process of writing requirements using the V-Model development life-cycle.

identifying how requirements should be allocated to specific system elements. The edge AI system elements can include hardware, software, AI, edge AI, GenAI, agentic AI and data. As these system elements are defined, additional requirement statements, known as derived requirements, must be created. These derived requirements specify relationships among architectural elements, provide clarity at lower levels of abstraction, and define specific design constraints or performance levels. This allocation and derivation are accomplished through the recursive application of requirements definition processes. The process of writing requirements when using the V-Model development life-cycle is illustrated in Figure 3.1.

In this context, the principles of requirements engineering, as outlined in ISO/IEC/IEEE 29148:2018 and the accompanying text, can provide a structured framework for managing the complexity of edge AI systems.

Certain requirements cannot be derived until specific portions of the architecture or design have evolved. Many requirements depend heavily on the interoperation and interoperability of multiple edge AI system elements. The information throughput of edge systems depends on the complex interactions among system hardware, software, AI algorithms, frameworks, data, datasets and the operational environment. To capture the elements effectively, the requirements, architecture, and design processes must be applied recursively and iteratively. The flow for transferring edge AI system requirements into subsystem requirements, system architecture, and design is illustrated in Figure 3.2.

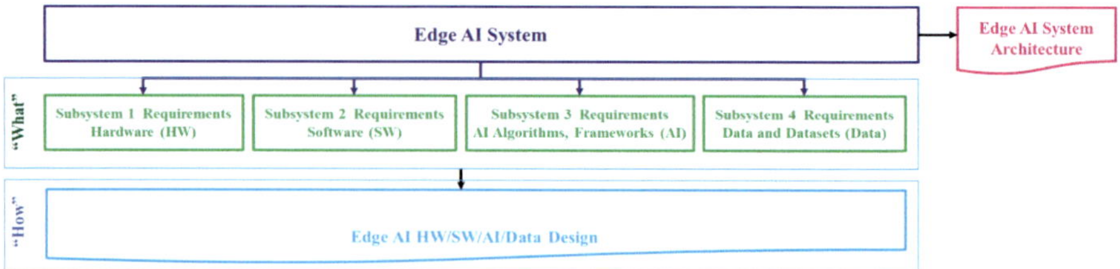

Figure 3.2 Edge AI system requirements flow into subsystem requirements, architecture and design.

Even in scenarios where requirements engineering is well-resourced, the level of analysis is seldom applied uniformly across the entire edge AI system. Experienced engineers can often identify early in the process where existing or off-the-shelf solutions can be adapted for specific edge AI system elements. As a result, requirements allocated to the standard elements may require less analysis. In contrast, elements where the solution is less obvious, or novel, require further, more detailed analysis. Critical requirements, those involving high risk or impacting public safety, the environment, or health, must always be subjected to the most rigorous analysis.

Requirements processes, and their resulting specifications depend on the scope of the system being defined. Requirements for a system or element are always subject to higher-level requirements regarding business operations. These requirements are allocated progressively to lower-level edge AI systems. A representation of the requirements scope in a business context is illustrated in Figure 3.3.

The hierarchy of specifications generally includes several key documents (ISO/IEC/IEEE 29148:2018). The business requirements specification represents business management levels, while the stakeholder requirements specification represents business operational levels. These flow down into the system requirements specification. At the technical implementation level, specific documents are generated, including the edge AI system requirements specification, hardware requirements specification software requirements specification, AI algorithms, frameworks requirements specification, and data and datasets requirements specification. The information items can be applied to multiple specifications iteratively or recursively.

The system requirements and the edge AI system requirements specifications are critical documents that identifies the technical requirements for the system-of-interest and defines the usability of system interaction. It outlines high-level requirements from a domain perspective, including objectives,

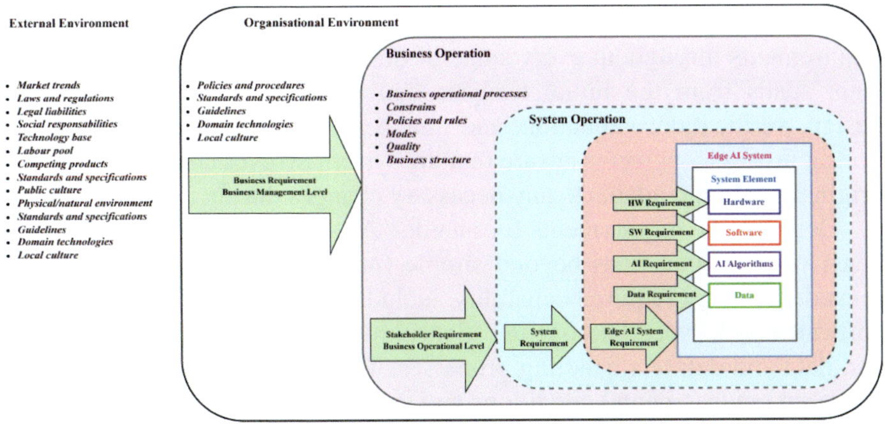

Figure 3.3 Requirements scope in a business context (Adapted from ISO/IEC/IEEE 29148:2018).

the target environment, constraints, assumptions, and non-functional requirements. It may also utilise conceptual models to illustrate system context, usage scenarios, entities, data, and workflows.

The primary purpose of the system requirements specification is to provide a description of how the system should interact with its external environment. It must completely describe all inputs, outputs, and their relationships. The system requirements specification serves as a bridge between the user and the technical community. The requirements collection in the specification must be understandable to both groups.

A distinction should be made between the structured collection of requirement information and its presentation to various stakeholders (e.g., users, data scientists, embedded engineers, etc.). The presentation of the system requirements specification should take a form appropriate for its intended use, whether as a paper document, models, prototypes, or a combination thereof. All presentations must be traceable to a common source of information to avoid ambiguity.

Generally, process requirements for developing or constructing the system should be documented in the contract, such as a statement of work, rather than in the requirements specification. If they are included in the specification, they must be clearly identified as process requirements. The system requirements specification ultimately documents the results of the need definition, operational concept, system architecture, and requirements analysis tasks, describing the acquirer's expectations for performance, quality, and verification.

The life cycle of an edge AI system demands rigorous monitoring of requirements throughout every stage of development. This continuous oversight spans from the initial analysis and specification phases through to design, verification, validation, and final testing. By maintaining this monitoring process, engineers ensure that the system evolves consistently with its original goals and adapts to any necessary changes during its development.

Defining the requirements for an edge AI system necessitates a comprehensive scope that goes beyond simple functionality. These specifications must detail every required capability, including the underlying hardware, the software stack, specific edge AI algorithms, chosen edge AI frameworks, and data and datasets handling processes. The requirements must document the exact environmental conditions and constraints under which the edge AI system is expected to operate, ensuring the technology is robust enough for its real-world application.

A critical component of this process is requirements verification, which focuses on the quality and structure of the specifications themselves. This involves a systematic examination to confirm that each requirement, both individually and as part of a collective set, is well-formed. The verification process reviews these specifications to ensure they exhibit the characteristics of high-quality requirements, such as clarity and consistency, that the requirements are necessary, verifiable, achievable and that the entire set is logically organised.

Complementing verification is requirements validation, which ensures alignment with user needs. Validation confirms that the requirements, whether viewed in isolation or as a complete package, accurately define the "right" edge AI system. This step bridges the gap between technical specifications and stakeholder or user expectations, ensuring the intended design accurately reflects what users and stakeholders envisioned for the final solution.

The requirements documents must explicitly outline the intended approaches for verification, validation, and testing. By establishing testing protocols early in the requirements phase, developers create a clear roadmap for assessing the edge AI system's performance. This approach ensures that the hardware, software, edge AI algorithms, frameworks and data meet technical standards and function effectively within the specific constraints of the edge AI environment.

4

Edge AI Non-Functional Requirements

4.1 Definition

The field of edge AI is relatively new and there is no established standardised definition solely for edge AI system non-functional requirements (NFRs) provided by ISO or IEEE standards. This work intends to use the concepts associated with NFRs for edge AI systems using broader concepts of systems based on the existing hardware, software, AI components and data engineering. These concepts guide specifying non-functional requirements that can be adapted to edge AI environments' unique characteristics and constraints.

While no standard exclusively defines edge AI non-functional requirements, ISO and IEEE standards such as ISO/IEC/IEEE 29148:2018 [55], IEEE 2874-2025 [186], and ISO/IEC 25010:2023 [45] provide robust frameworks for understanding and specifying these requirements. Non-functional requirements are essential for ensuring that a system performs correctly and meets broader quality and operational demands, aligning with stakeholder expectations and regulatory constraints.

The ISO/IEC/IEEE 29148:2018 [55] standard defines non-functional requirements as quality requirements that include several of the ilities' in requirements, for example, reliability, usability, security, compatibility, reusability, scalability, maintainability, flexibility, safety, and portability. The kinds of quality requirements (e.g., "ilities") should be identified prior to initiating the requirements activities. This should be tailored to the system(s) being developed. As appropriate, measures for meeting the quality requirements should also be included. Additional guidance on software quality requirements can be found in the ISO/IEC SQuaRE standards, particularly ISO/IEC 25030:2019 [53], as well as in ISO/IEC 25010:2023 [45] and IEEE 2874-2025 [186]. A summary of the product quality model characteristics presented in ISO/IEC 25010:2023 is shown in Table 4.2, which includes characteristics such as functional suitability, performance efficiency, compatibility, interaction capability, as well as reliability, security, maintainability, flexibility, and safety with several specific sub-characteristics.

DOI: 10.1201/9788743809586-4

In the design of edge AI systems, NFRs, or quality requirements are the primary architectural drivers that dictate the system's design and feasibility. The convergence of AI's probabilistic nature with the severe constraints of edge computing creates a new and complex landscape of quality attributes that must be proper engineered.

Many traditional NFRs are intensified in the edge AI context, becoming more critical and challenging to satisfy. Performance, often measured in terms of latency and throughput, is paramount for the real-time applications that edge AI enables. Energy efficiency is a critical constraint for battery-powered or thermally limited devices, directly impacting their operational lifespan and viability. Reliability and availability are essential, as edge AI systems must often function autonomously and dependably, even with intermittent network connectivity. Security and privacy take on new dimensions; physically accessible edge devices are exposed to novel threats, including direct attacks on the edge AI models (e.g., data poisoning, adversarial evasion), while the local processing of data introduces new challenges in preventing information leakage.

Edge AI introduces a new class of emergent quality attributes that are central to a system's trustworthiness and social acceptance. Model accuracy, including measurements like precision and recall, is a quality that must be specified and measured. Robustness, the model's ability to maintain performance in the presence of noisy or adversarial inputs, is critical for real-world deployment. Explainability (XAI), the capacity to provide human-understandable reasons for a model's decision, is an increasingly vital requirement for user trust, debugging, and regulatory compliance. Fairness and the mitigation of bias are crucial ethical and legal requirements, ensuring that the edge AI models do not make systematically discriminatory decisions. Adaptability and retrainability refer to the system's capacity to evolve in response to changing data distributions (concept drift) over time, often through on-device or federated learning techniques.

The edge AI NFR landscape is a multi-layered construct as quality attributes apply to different parts of the edge AI system and a detailed approach requires decomposing NFRs and specifying them for distinct scopes: the data (e.g., quality, completeness, lack of bias), the edge AI model (e.g., accuracy, robustness, fairness), the hardware and software platform (e.g., performance, energy efficiency), and the overall system-in-operation (e.g., reliability, security, privacy). This multi-scope view is essential for effective requirements management and trade-off analysis. Edge AI system

NFRs refer to the criteria describing how a system operates rather than specific behaviours or functions. These requirements define an edge AI system's quality attributes and characteristics, performance benchmarks, and constraints, encompassing functional suitability, performance efficiency, compatibility, interaction capability, reliability, security, maintainability, flexibility, and safety [55].

Capturing non-functional requirements is critical to ensuring edge AI systems meet necessary quality and performance standards. Non-functional requirements in this context focus on "how" an edge AI system performs its functions, providing detailed specifications for quality attributes.

4.2 Methodology for Defining NFRs

The process of engineering edge AI systems is an exercise in making reasoned trade-offs between numerous conflicting NFRs and constraints. To manage the complexity, qualitative goals must be translated into quantitative, verifiable requirements. For example, an imprecise goal like "the system should be energy efficient" must be specified as "under operational load A, the system's average power consumption shall not exceed 100 mW". In the same manner, an ethical goal like "the edge AI model should be fair" must be quantified as "the edge AI model's false positive rate for demographic group A shall not differ from that of group B by more than a specified percentage on benchmark dataset Z".

This quantification enables structured trade-off analysis, which is an important design activity in edge AI. However, it is not possible to simultaneously maximise all desirable qualities, such as achieving the highest accuracy with the lowest latency and the minimum power consumption and therefore, the engineering goal is not maximisation but optimisation to find the best possible compromise that satisfies the most critical requirement within the given constraints.

Several key trade-off axes dominate edge AI system design. The most common trade-off is between model accuracy and system performance (latency and throughput), where more complex and accurate models are inherently slower and more resource-intensive. This is managed through techniques like model compression and hardware acceleration. Another critical axis is performance versus energy consumption, which is addressed through hardware-software co-design and power management techniques.

Table 4.1 Trade-off analyses in edge AI system design

Trade-off	**Conflicting NFRs**	**Design considerations**	**Management techniques**
Model Complexity	Accuracy vs. Latency, Memory Footprint, Energy consumption	Target hardware's compute/memory capacity. Real-time performance requirements. Power budget.	Model Pruning, Quantization, Knowledge Distillation, Neural Architecture Search (NAS), HW-SW Co-design.
Computational Efficiency	Performance (Latency/ Throughput) vs. Energy Consumption	Thermal design power (TDP) of the device. Battery life requirements. Required responsiveness of the application.	HW Acceleration (GPU, NPU, FPGA), Hardware-Software Co-design, Dynamic Voltage and Frequency Scaling (DVFS), Efficient algorithm-to-hardware mapping.
Data Management	Privacy vs. Model Accuracy/Adaptability	Regulatory requirements (e.g., GDPR). Need for model personalisation and continuous improvement. Network bandwidth availability.	Federated Learning, Differential Privacy, On-device training, Data minimisation and anonymisation techniques.
System Security	Security vs. Performance, Cost	Threat model, including physical access and model-specific attacks. Resource cost of cryptographic operations and security monitoring.	Trusted execution environments (TEEs), Lightweight cryptography, HW Security Modules (HSMs), Adversarial training, Model obfuscation.

Another example of a trade-off is that enhancing an edge AI model's robustness against adversarial attacks may require a more complex architecture, negatively impacting efficiency in federated learning. Table 4.1 provides a set of examples for trade-off analyses in edge AI system design.

To navigate this multi-dimensional design space, engineers can employ formal methods for trade-off analysis. Creating Pareto frontiers, which are a set of optimal solutions that strike a balance between revenue maximisation and cost minimisation in the design and scheduling, allows for the visualisation of optimal solutions for multi-objective problems, showing the set

Table 4.2 ISO/IEC 25010:2023 [45] overview, including characteristics and sub-characteristics

Software product quality				
Functional suitability	**Performance efficiency**	**Compatibility**	**Interaction capability**	
Functional completeness. Functional correctness. Functional appropriateness.	Time behaviour. Resource utilization. Capacity.	Co-existence. Interoperability.	Appropriateness recognizability. Learnability. Operability. User error protection. User engagement. Inclusivity. User assistance. Self-descriptive.	
Reliability	**Security**	**Maintainability**	**Flexibility**	**Safety**
Faultlessness. Availability. Fault tolerance. Recoverability.	Confidentiality. Integrity. Non-repudiation. Accountability. Authenticity. Resistance.	Modularity. Reusability. Analysability. Modifiable. Testability.	Adaptability. Scalability. Instability. Replaceability.	Operational constraint. Risk identification. Fail safe. Hazard warning. Safe integration.

of designs that offer the best possible accuracy for a given latency budget. Quantitative frameworks can also be used to structure the decision-making process by weighting different NFRs according to priorities, ensuring that trade-offs are made consciously and defensibly. This continuous process of co-design and co-optimisation across the entire system stack, data, edge AI model, software, and hardware, is the essence of engineering edge AI.

The NFRs can be mapped to the ISO/IEC 25010:2023 attributes or characteristics and sub-characteristics for edge AI systems and data quality requirements in ISO/IEC 25012:2008 [46].

A summary of the product quality model characteristics presented in ISO/IEC 25010:2023 is shown in Table 4.2.

Each NFR has a KPI identified and a measure to provide a verifiable and quantifiable (qualitative/quantitative) assessment. The methodology proposed is based on the measures described in ISO/IEC 25023:2016 [51] and ISO/IEC 25021:2012 [49] (parts of the ISO/IEC 25000:2014 and series of standards [171, 172] SQuaRE series - System and software quality requirements and evaluation) as reference.

The role of ISO/IEC 25000 in measuring and assessing AI product quality is widely recognised and has received increasing interest, as the standards propose measurement methods like those developed in scientific literature and projects, aligning with the ISO 25000 conforming measurement method [133]. The work in [133] analysed this similarity and concluded that most measurement methods used for AI can be easily mapped into the ISO 25000 format.

The ISO/IEC 25012:2008 standard can be used in edge AI systems to extend the product quality model defined in ISO/IEC 25010:2023 with the data properties. The standard covers data held in a structured format, and it specifies a general data quality model. The target is data processed or stored by the system which can be considered persistent data. Conformance of data to a data design specification is outside the scope of the standard. Data quality is the degree to which data properties satisfy explicit and implicit needs when used in a specified context. The quality is intended to be application-dependent. It does not consider universal data quality that can be applied for any purpose.

Data quality characteristics are defined as the attributes that affect quality. ISO/IEC 25012:2008 defines data quality through two main categories: inherent data quality and system-dependent data quality. These categories encompass fifteen data quality characteristics, five for inherent data quality (accuracy, completeness, consistency, credibility, currentness) and ten for system-dependent data quality (accessibility, compliance, confidentiality, efficiency, precision, traceability, understandability, availability, portability, recoverability).

The IEEE Global Initiative on Ethics of Autonomous and Intelligent Systems [78] highlighted in 2016 the importance of integrating socio-technical standards early in development to ensure that autonomous and intelligent systems align with human values, intentions, and understanding, thereby reducing the risk of unwanted behaviours. These standards are informed by IEEE's Ethically-Aligned Design P7000 Series of standards that address human rights, well-being, accountability, and transparency for AI and autonomous intelligent systems.

In response to this initiative, the Spatial Web Foundation [79] and the IEEE P2874 Spatial Web, Architecture, and Governance Working Group [80] have developed the IEEE P2874 standards, including the Spatial Web Protocol, Architecture, and Governance specifications. These specifications, approved and ratified by IEEE in May 2025, define the system requirements for the interoperability and governance of cyber-physical systems, encompassing autonomous devices, applications, spatial content, and operations. Networked communication systems designed to meet these specifications enable the standardised representation of statements, relationships, interactions in the physical and digital sociotechnical systems, making them suitable for computational modelling, simulation, and automation.

The design and development of edge AI systems need to embed AI trustworthiness concepts. These encompass several aspects addressed by system engineering dependability that include several system quality properties (e.g., security, safety, availability, connectability, resilience, reliability, maintainability, and privacy) covered by ISO/IEC TS 5723:2022 in addition to ISO/IEC 25010:2023 and ISO/IEC 25012:2008.

The further development of edge AI systems includes ethical edge AI considerations (e.g., fairness, responsibility, accountability, governance) and specific (e.g., explainability, interpretability) that are intrinsic to the data-centric and black-box nature of ML/DL edge AI.

An extensive list of quality attributes or characteristics that can be used as NFRs for edge AI systems is given below.

- **Functional suitability** represents the degree to which a product or system provides functions that meet stated and implied needs when used under specified conditions. This characteristic is formed by sub-characteristics functional completeness, functional correctness, functional appropriateness.
- **Performance efficiency** reflects the performance relative to the resources used under stated conditions. This characteristic is formed by sub-characteristics of time behaviour, resource utilisation, and capacity.
- **Compatibility** is the degree to which a product, system or component can exchange information with other products, systems, or components and/or perform its required functions while sharing the same hardware or software environment. This characteristic is composed of sub-characteristics of co-existence and interoperability.
- **Interaction capability** is the degree to which a product or system can be interacted with by specified users to exchange information in the user interface to complete specific tasks in a variety of contexts of use. This characteristic is composed of the following sub-characteristics appropriateness recognizability, learnability, operability, user error protection, user engagement, user assistance, self-descriptiveness.

- **Reliability** is the degree to which a system, product or component performs specified functions under specified conditions for a specified period of time. This characteristic comprises sub-characteristics of faultlessness, availability, fault tolerance, and recoverability. Reliability is the system ability of an item to perform as required, without failure, for a given time interval, under given conditions. The time interval duration can be expressed in units appropriate to the item concerned (e.g. calendar time, operating cycles, distance run, etc.) and the units should always be clearly stated. The conditions include aspects that affect reliability, such as mode of operation, stress levels, environmental conditions, and maintenance (IEC 60050-192:2015 [185]).
- **Security** is the degree to which a product or system protects information and data so that persons or other products or systems have the degree of data access appropriate to their types and levels of authorisation. The authorisation comprises sub-characteristics confidentiality, integrity, non-repudiation, accountability, authenticity and resistance. Security represents the degree of resistance to intentional, unauthorised act(s) designed to cause harm or damage to an edge A *system* (ISO/IEC 23643:2020 [173]).
- **Maintainability** represents the degree of effectiveness and efficiency with which a product or system can be modified to improve it, correct it, or adapt it to changes in the environment and requirements. This characteristic comprises sub-characteristics modularity, reusability, analysability, modifiability, and testability.
- **Flexibility** is the degree to which a product can be adapted to changes in its requirements, contexts of use or system environment. This characteristic is composed of sub-characteristics adaptability, scalability, installability, and replaceability.
- **Safety** represents the degree to which a product under defined conditions to avoid a state in which human life, health, property, or the environment is endangered. This characteristic is composed of sub-characteristics operational constraint, risk identification, fail safe, hazard warning and safe integration. Safety is the property of an edge AI *system* such that it does not, under defined conditions, lead to a state in which human life, health, property, or the environment is endangered (ISO/IEC/IEEE 12207:2017 [56]).
- **Accountability** relates to an allocated responsibility, which can be based on regulation or agreement or through assignment as part of delegation.

Accountability is a property that ensures that an entity's actions can be traced uniquely to the entity (ISO 7498-2:1989 [174]). In the context of edge AI, accountability is the obligation of the producer of the edge AI system to account for its system or services and disclose the results transparently if needed. The responsibility for the edge AI's action/inaction/malfunction is attributed to an actor that is part of a business agreement, the owner, designer/developer, manufacturer, operator of an edge AI technology or application.

- **Governance** refers to the framework of norms, laws, and regulations that guide the development, deployment, and use of artificial intelligence within a specific domain. It encompasses the principles and standards that ensure AI systems operate ethically, transparently, and responsibly, aligning with societal values and legal requirements. It seeks to establish accountability and protect rights while preventing harm and mitigating risks associated with their application.
- **Accuracy** is a measure of the closeness of results of observations, computations, or estimates to the true values or the values accepted as being true (ISO 17572-1:2022, 3.1 [175]).
- **Authenticity** is a property that an entity is what it claims to be (ISO/IEC 27000:2018, 3.6 [176]).
- **Availability** is the property of being accessible and usable on demand by an authorised entity (ISO/IEC 27000:2018, 3.7).
- **Spatiability** refers to the capability of representing information as locations and relationships within a hyperspace to structure and interpret data. The spatial representation allows intelligent computing systems to perform tasks and make decisions based on spatio-temporal context (IEEE 2874-2025).
- **Controllability** is the property of an AI *system* that allows a human or another external agent to intervene in the edge AI system's functioning (ISO/IEC 22989:2022, 3.5.6 [21]).
- **Integrity** is a property whereby data have not been altered in an unauthorised manner since they were created, transmitted, or stored (ISO/IEC 29167-19:2019, 3.3 [177]). Integrity can be a system property of *accuracy* and completeness (ISO/IEC 27000:2018, 3.36).
- **Privacy** is the freedom from intrusion into the private life or affairs of an individual (ISO/IEC 2382:2015, 2.22).

- **Resilience** is the *capability* of an edge AI *system* to maintain its functions and structure in the face of internal and external change and to degrade gracefully when this is necessary.
- **Robustness** is the ability of an edge AI *system* to maintain its level of performance under a variety of circumstances (ISO/IEC 22989:2022). Robustness is the ability of edge AI systems to maintain their performance when faced with various challenges, such as perturbations, unexpected changes or adversarial and malicious inputs. This quality attribute or characteristic of edge AI systems encompasses two key aspects: algorithm robustness, which evaluates the learning algorithm's resilience to variations in the training dataset, and model robustness, which assesses how well a trained model withstands alterations and perturbations in input data.
- **Transparency** is the property of an edge AI system or process to imply openness and *accountability* (ISO/IEC 27036-3:2023 [178]). Transparency relates to the capability of an edge AI system to, always, be able to provide a satisfactory explanation for its decisions, auditable either by an in-house or an independent human authority assessment. In the case of failure causing harm, it should be possible to ascertain why.
- **Usability** represents the extent to which an edge AI *system,* product, or service can be used by specified users to achieve specified goals with effectiveness, efficiency, and satisfaction in a specified context (ISO 9241-11:2018 [179]).
- **Fairness** represents the extent to ensure mechanisms embedded in guidelines and initiatives related to ethics, bias mitigation, and responsible edge AI technology development. Edge AI fairness is discussed in terms like bias mitigation to ensure that edge AI algorithms and datasets do not produce or perpetuate bias, equitability to ensure edge AI systems treat all users fairly, transparency to provide clarity on how edge AI systems make decisions and accountability to ensure that edge AI systems are held responsible for their outcomes. Fairness in edge AI can be context-dependent and subject to varying interpretations based on cultural, social, and legal factors.
- **Explainability** is the ability to explain the decision-making process in terms that are understandable to the end user. An explainable model provides a clear and intuitive explanation of the decisions made, enabling users to understand why the model has produced a particular result;

it focuses on why an algorithm has made a specific decision and how that decision can be justified. It requires a straightforward and intuitive presentation of information using an ontology familiar to the user. It is particularly valuable and beneficial in the case of deep neural networks, where the models are difficult to interpret due to the convoluted structure and complex internal interactions. Explainability is a consideration of the deployed AI model.

- **Interpretability** is the ability to understand the decision-making process of an edge AI model. An interpretable edge AI model provides clear information about the relationship between inputs and outputs. An interpretable algorithm can be explained clearly and understandably by a person. Interpretability is essential to ensure that users will trust AI models. Interpretability is mostly associated with model training, evaluation, and quality assurance.

Using the information provided in [45] non-functional requirements for edge AI systems are specifying how well the functionality should present itself and behave, aligning to the other quality characteristics outlined in ISO/IEC 25010:2023 System and software quality models, ISO/IEC 25012:2008 Data quality model and specific AI quality attributes or characteristics. Non-functional requirements are related to some, or all the functionality and typically functional requirements are associated with appropriate non-functional requirements, either individually or in groups.

The non-functional requirements for edge AI systems can have a two-layer representation following the ISO/IEC 25010:2023 model with a "high-level" non-functional requirement assigned to the quality characteristics or attributes and a "low-level" non-functional requirement assigned to the quality sub-characteristics or attributes.

Table 4.3 provides a set of examples for the comparison between the traditional NFRs and the AI-centric ones.

4.3 Edge AI Non-Functional Requirements, Key KPIs and Measures.

The following section provides examples (structured in tables) of edge AI non-functional requirements, KPIs, and measures that researchers and practitioners can use as references for their projects. The examples cover various areas of application.

Table 4.3 Comparison of traditional and AI-centric NFRs

NFR Category	**Traditional System Context**	**Edge AI System Context and Key Measures**
Performance	Response time, throughput, resource utilisation.	**Latency:** Inference time (ms). **Throughput:** Inferences per second (IPS). **Energy:** Joules per inference.
Reliability	Mean Time Between Failures (MTBF), availability (uptime percentage).	Includes traditional metrics plus model stability and graceful degradation under data drift or noisy inputs.
Security	Network security (firewalls, IDS), access control, data encryption.	Includes traditional aspects plus model-specific vulnerabilities. Metrics include resilience to model inversion, membership inference, data poisoning, and adversarial evasion attacks. Physical device security is critical.
Privacy	Data protection compliance (e.g., GDPR), anonymisation of stored data.	Enhanced by on-device processing. Challenges include preventing data leakage during federated learning or model updates. Compliance with data minimisation principles.
Explainability	New type of NFR. System logic is documented in specifications.	A critical emergent NFR. Measured by techniques like LIME/SHAP scores, rule extraction fidelity, or qualitative user studies on explanation clarity.
Fairness	New type of NFR. Assumed to be handled by business logic.	A critical ethical and legal NFR. Measured by statistical parity, equal opportunity, or equalised odds across demographic groups on benchmark datasets.
Robustness	Fault tolerance, graceful degradation to HW/SW faults.	Model's resilience to perturbations in input data. Measured by accuracy drop on corrupted or adversarial datasets (e.g., Projected Gradient Descent-PGD attacks).
Adaptability	System's ability to be modified for new requirements (maintainability, extensibility).	Model's ability to adapt to concept/data drift over time. Measured by performance retention after on-device retraining or federated learning cycles.

4.3.1 Performance Efficiency

Table 4.4 Performance efficiency (Time-behaviour)

NFR aspect	**NFR description**
Name	Characteristics: **Performance efficiency** Sub-Characteristics: **Time-behaviour**
Definition	System frame rate.
Description	Frame rate.
What is measured	How many predictions the system can perform per unit of time.
KPI	System throughput.
Methods of collection/ measurement and verification/validation	Measurement of inference time on a realistic use-case configuration (e.g., same data format, same system configuration) in various task-related conditions (e.g., night, light for the external camera).
Target Value	Given number of sample per seconds (e.g., frame/s, token/s, sample/s).

Table 4.5 Performance efficiency (Resource utilization)

NFR aspect	**NFR description**
Name	Characteristics: **Performance efficiency** Sub-Characteristics: **Resource utilization**
Definition	System power consumption.
Description	Power consumption.
What is measured	How much the edge AI system consume power while used on raw sensor data.
KPI	Power consumption.
Methods of collection/ measurement and verification/validation	Inference in real-use conditions. Power measurement on various scenes and conditions.
Target Value	A given/max value of power consumption [mW] (e.g., 50 mW).

Table 4.6 Performance efficiency (Resource utilization)

NFR aspect	**NFR description**
Name	Characteristics: **Performance efficiency** Sub-Characteristics: **Resource utilization**
Definition	System memory consumption
Description	Memory consumption
What is measured	How much memory is required by the edge AI system, and the related AI model.
KPI	Memory
Methods of collection/ measurement and verification/validation	Static requirements for storing model parameters and monitoring dynamic memory needs for execution.
Target Value	A given/max value of memory use [MB] (e.g., $<$ 2MB).

Table 4.7 Performance efficiency (Capacity)

NFR aspect	NFR description
Name	Characteristic: **Performance efficiency** Sub-characteristics: **Capacity**
Definition	Degree to which the maximum limits of a product or system parameter meet requirements.
Description	The system capacity of handling many requests, data or events.
What is measured	Maximum volume of events or data that can be processed by the system/edge system.
KPI	Highest number of requests (data units, event units, messages units) that the system can handle without significant failure (failure to answer, wrong response, delayed response).
Methods of collection/ measurement and verification/validation	Counting the volume of requests in units. Stress test with typical data in operational conditions.
Target Value	Number of user requests processing at the same time (depends on the system) (e.g., processing 1000 user requests simultaneously).

4.3.2 Compatibility

Table 4.8 Compatibility (Co-existence)

NFR aspect	NFR description
Name	Characteristic: **Compatibility** Sub-characteristics: **Co-existence**
Definition	Co-existence of SSMA and existing equipment methods. Co- existence of developed methods with other existing methods consume the same HW and data source → degree to which a product can perform its required functions efficiently while sharing a common environment and resources with other products, without detrimental impact on any other product.
Description	Co- existence of developed methods with other existing methods consume the same HW and data source. • Understanding of computational resources • Finding out limitations and opportunities
What is measured	RAM on the computational resource, connection latency on other existing methods, usage of CPU.
KPI	Utilization of resources.
Methods of collection/ measurement and verification/validation	Tracking of existing computational resources via existing dashboard. Verification: deployment on test environment. Validation: Comparison of resources w/o running and w/running inference/ training.
Target Value	The average utilization increases less than a given percentage [%] of the available resources depending on inference or training (e.g., average utilization increases less than 50% of the available resources).

Table 4.9 Compatibility (Interoperability)

NFR aspect	NFR description
Domain example	Digital industry domain.
Name	Characteristic: **Compatibility** Sub-characteristics: **Interoperability**
Definition	Interoperability of the SSMA - method(s). What are the constrains where all systems competing for, internally and externally.
Description	Degree to which two or more decision making systems, products or components can exchange information/knowledge and use the information/knowledge that has been exchanged.
What is measured	Number of downstream systems that leverage the results of these models. • Response time for inference on downstream system. • Generalization of the model results. flexibility of the deployment environment (e.g., different frameworks – Keras, TensorFlow, etc.).
KPI	Number of use cases which the model results can be used for. Number of different deployment environment which the model can be host in.
Methods of collection/ measurement and verification/ validation	Develop testing framework to measure inference response time on downstream tasks and test different deployment env. that mimics the actual production line. Count use cases per model. Verification: deployment on test environment.
Target Value	Response time value.

4.3.3 Interaction Capability

Table 4.10 Interaction capability (Learnability)

NFR aspect	NFR description
Name	Characteristics: **Interaction capability** Sub-Characteristics: **Learnability**
Definition	Ensure learnability by ensuring a user-friendly interface and intuitive control for user.
Description	Provision of self-explanatory user interface with intuitive controls, and status of temperature and time-capability of warm water delivery.
What is measured	User satisfaction rating.
KPI	Usability score on a defined scale (e.g., ranging from 1 to 10).
Methods of collection/ measurement and verification/ validation	Let various persons tyre the interface, observe time spend to perform some common functions. Measure task success rate and time on task. Usability test with a defined number of different people related to the company, measuring task success rate and time on task. Record the values.
Target Value	A predefined minimum score according to the given scale. (E.g., target value to be at least 8 on a scale from 1 to 10).

Table 4.11 Interaction capability (User error protection)

NFR aspect	**NFR description**
Name	Characteristics: **Interaction capability** Sub-Characteristics: **User error protection**
Definition	Degree to which a system protects users against making errors.
Description	The end-user should not be required to provide a manual input to obtain a prediction result, which eliminates the possibility of user errors.
What is measured	Number of manual inputs required by the end user.
KPI	End-user manual inputs.
Methods of collection/ measurement and verification/ validation	Analysis of system architecture. Testing by end-users.
Target Value	The number maximum acceptable manual inputs required (e.g., 0 (none)).

Table 4.12 Interaction capability (User engagement)

NFR aspect	**NFR description**
Name	Characteristic: **Interaction capability** Sub-characteristics: **User engagement**
Definition	Degree to which a user interface presents functions and information in an inviting and motivating manner encouraging continued interaction.
Description	The use of the device or system should de motivating for human users to keep them engaged with the system.
What is measured	Average session duration, user retention rate, interaction frequency.
KPI	Duration of a session in minutes, return rate of identified users, number of interactions per minute.
Methods of collection/ measurement and verification/ validation	Automatic collection in the log file of the system. Analysis of the log files and measure of the above-mentioned KPIs.
Target Value	Session duration greater than a given time [min], retention greater than a given rate [%], and number of interactions per minute (e.g., session time $>$ 20 minutes, retention $>$ 30%, 3-5 interactions per minute).

Table 4.13 Interaction capability (Inclusivity)

NFR aspect	**NFR description**
Name	Characteristic: **Interaction capability** Sub-characteristics: **Inclusivity**
Definition	Degree to which a product or system can be used by people of various backgrounds (such as people of various ages, abilities, cultures, ethnicities, languages, genders, economic situations, etc.).
Description	The system should avoid barriers for people with various backgrounds
What is measured	The extent to which the system is usable from a large portion of the population.
KPI	Number of supported languages in the interface, visibility/contrast of user interface, possibility of use with disabilities
Methods of collection/ measurement and verification/ validation	Analysis of the user interface, user satisfaction survey on usability for specific populations. Analysis of the system and counting the elements or conduction of a user study with a given number of users from a specific background.
Target Value	Number of supported languages their satisfaction score target value. (E.g., supported languages $>$ 8, satisfaction score $>$ 8 out of 10).

Table 4.14 Interaction capability (User assistance)

NFR aspect	**NFR description**
Name	Characteristic: **Interaction capability** Sub-characteristics: **User assistance**
Definition	Degree to which a product can be used by people with the widest range of characteristics and capabilities to achieve specified goals in a specified context of use.
Description	System should be accessible with different means to cover differences in abilities from the users.
What is measured	Capacity of accomplishing the desired goal in presence of disabilities.
KPI	Number of input/output methods proposed for interacting with the system (voice, typing, sound etc.).
Methods of collection/ measurement and verification/ validation	Analysis of the system in terms of number of interaction possibilities. Test run with various input/output methods.
Target Value	Number of available interacting (input/output methods) alternatives. (E.g., the system should offer at least 2 alternatives for interacting).

Table 4.15 Interaction capability (Self-descriptive)

NFR aspect	**NFR description**
Name	Characteristic: **Interaction Capability** Sub-characteristics: **Self-descriptive**
Definition	Degree to which a product presents appropriate information, where needed by the user, to make its capabilities and use immediately obvious to the user without excessive interactions with a product or other resources (such as user documentation, help desks or other users).
Description	The system should contain enough information to be used without referring to documentation.
What is measured	Ease of interaction and clarity of what is happening and how to interact.
KPI	User satisfaction with the interaction with the system.
Methods of collection/ measurement and verification/ validation	Running tests with selected users and evaluate satisfaction with an adequate feedback form. User satisfaction survey with a defined minimum of users.
Target Value	A predefined minimum satisfaction level score according to the given scale (e.g., satisfaction level of 8 on a scale from 1 to 10).

4.3.4 Reliability

Table 4.16 Reliability (Availability)

NFR aspect	**NFR description**
Name	Characteristics: **Reliability** Sub-Characteristics: **Availability**
Definition	Degree to which a system, product or component is operational and accessible when required for use.
Description	High reliability is key for eventual use in productive environment: Ideally, each measurement in the production line should correspond to a prediction.
What is measured	Number of measurements in the production line, number of predictions done.
KPI	Ratio of predicted lots to measured lots.
Methods of collection/ measurement and verification/ validation	Semi-automated comparison of equipment tracking data and prediction output. Data analysis.
Target Value	The minimum ration of predicted lots to measured lots given in percentages [%]. (E.g., ≥ 75 %).

Table 4.17 Reliability (Availability)

NFR aspect	NFR description
Name	Characteristics: **Reliability** Sub-Characteristics: **Availability**
Definition	Degree to which a system, product or component is operational and accessible when required for use in a specified period.
Description	Energy management system availability and mean downtime.
What is measured	The occurrence of system downtime for a specified period of time.
KPI	Qualitative [%].
Methods of collection/ measurement and verification/ validation	Demonstrator evaluation. Validation of availability/downtime parameters.
Target Value	System availability versus downtime given in percentages [%] (e.g., availability $\geq$ 90 %).

Table 4.18 Reliability (Fault tolerance)

NFR aspect	NFR description
Name	Characteristic: **Reliability** Sub-characteristics: **Fault tolerance**
Definition	Degree to which a system, product or component operates as intended despite the presence of hardware or software faults.
Description	The system should continue to provide the expected output when a software or hardware fault arises.
What is measured	Correspondence between provided output and expected output in presence of known faults.
KPI	The difference between output and expected output.
Methods of collection/ measurement and verification/ validation	Depends on the output type (unit, quantity). Injection of faults and stress test, or system log to analyse the behaviour in occurrence of a natural fault.
Target Value	The difference (in percentage [%]) of real output versus expected output in presence of a specific hardware or software fault (e.g., less than 10 % difference with expected output in presence of a specific HW or SW fault).

Table 4.19 Reliability (Recoverability)

NFR aspect	NFR description
Name	Characteristic: **Reliability** Sub-characteristics: **Recoverability**
Definition	Degree to which, in the event of an interruption or a failure, a product or system can recover the data directly affected and re-establish the desired state of the system.
Description	Ability of the system to return to a functioning state after a failure happened and has been detected and corrected.
What is measured	Failover mechanism to ensure data is not lost or corrupted and maintenance of the expected service
KPI	Integrity of the data after failure, continuity of data processing despite network failure
Methods of collection/ measurement and verification/ validation	Simulation of failure or actual failure in controlled environment. Simulated or intentional failure injection.
Target Value	The maximum amount of data loss [MB], when continue functioning (e.g., amount of lost data is less than 1 MB, ability to continue function even if as much as 1 MB of data is lost).

4.3.5 Security

Table 4.20 Security (Confidentiality)

NFR aspect	NFR description
Name	Characteristic: **Security** Sub-characteristics: **Confidentiality**
Definition	Degree to which a product or system ensures that data are accessible only to those authorized to have access.
Description	Systems should implement mechanisms to prevent access to confidential data by unwanted entities (hackers/other users).
What is measured	Number of successful attacks in which confidential data is accessed
KPI	Attack success rate = number of successful attacks over total number of attacks in a fixed period of time.
Methods of collection/ measurement and verification/ validation	Log files on system attacks or simulated attacks. Measure on the log files and/or after simulation.
Target Value	Maximum attack success rate [%] for a defined period of time (e.g., attack success rate < 0.001 %).

Table 4.21 Security (Confidentiality)

NFR aspect	NFR description
Name	Characteristic: **Security** Sub-characteristics: **Confidentiality**
Definition	Degree to which a product or system ensures that data are accessible only to those authorized to have access.
Description	Systems should implement mechanisms to prevent access to confidential data by unwanted entities (hackers/other users).
What is measured	Attacker's capability to reconstruct confidential data.
KPI	Percentage of data samples or features per sample reconstructed by the attacker, quality of the reconstructed data/features.
Methods of collection/ measurement and verification/ validation	Log files on system attacks or simulated attacks. Measure on the log files and/or after simulation.
Target Value	Maximum percentage of data/features reconstructed, minimum reconstruction error for given attacker's capabilities.

Table 4.22 Security (Integrity)

NFR aspect	NFR description
Name	Characteristics: **Security** Sub-Characteristics: **Integrity**
Definition	Degree to which a system protects data so other systems and sub-systems can access and use the data.
Description	Data synchronization and transfer mechanisms must guarantee the integrity in terms of protecting exchanged data from being corrupted, and handle cases when a device has not had internet access for a period of time.
What is measured	Number of faults in a series of messages. Number of packets without encryption.
KPI	Number of failed requests in Apache Kafka Broker.
Methods of collection/ measurement and verification/ validation	Live demonstration.
Target Value	Maximum number of failed decrypted messages (e.g., failed decrypted messages < 2 per connection).

4.3.6 Maintainability

Table 4.23 Maintainability (Modularity)

NFR aspect	**NFR description**
Name	Characteristics: **Maintainability** Sub-Characteristics: **Modularity**
Definition	Management Framework capable of serving AI models and updating them as needed, as well as scaling up types of supported sensory input.
Description	To develop an efficient, scalable, and maintainable edge AI framework adaptable to various forms of sensory feedback.
What is measured	Downtime required for maintenance and updates.
KPI	Time required for maintenance and updates.
Methods of collection/ measurement and verification/ validation	Measurement of time during live deployment.
Target Value	Maximum downtime [min] required for maintenance and updates (e.g., under 30 minutes of downtime).

Table 4.24 Maintainability (Reusability)

NFR aspect	**NFR description**
Name	Characteristics: **Maintainability** Sub-Characteristics: **Reusability**
Definition	Degree to which an asset can be used in more than one system, or in building other assets.
Description	The architecture should not only support the current, but also future use-cases. Therefore, the main architectural building blocks (scripts, hardware, training methodology, ...) should be reusable.
What is measured	How many building blocks can be reused for future use-cases.
KPI	Ratio of re-used building blocks to total building blocks.
Methods of collection/ measurement and verification/ validation	Analysis of system architecture. Data analysis.
Target Value	The minimum number of re-used building blocks versus total building blocks given in percentages [%] (e.g., $\geq$ 60 %).

Table 4.25 Maintainability (Reusability)

NFR aspect	NFR description
Name	Characteristics: **Maintainability** Sub-Characteristics: **Reusability**
Definition	Degree to which the intelligent gateway can be used in more than one energy management system, or in building other systems.
Description	How efficient the gateways functional blocks can be used to other energy management system regarding reusability assets.
What is measured	The efficiency of the functional block used in different energy management applications.
KPI	Qualitative [%].
Methods of collection/ measurement and verification/ validation	Demonstrator evaluation. Validation of reusability.
Target Value	The degree (in percentage [%]) of reusing the intelligent gateway in other energy management systems or in building other management systems. (e.g., at least 80 % reusability).

Table 4.26 Maintainability (Analysability)

NFR aspect	NFR description
Name	Characteristic: **Maintainability** Sub-characteristics: **Analysability**
Definition	Degree of effectiveness and efficiency with which it is possible to assess the impact on a product or system of an intended change to one or more of its parts, to diagnose a product for deficiencies or causes of failures, or to identify parts to be modified.
Description	The extent to which a system can be understood when planning an extension of searching for causes of failures.
What is measured	Readability and understandability of code, documentation of hardware, documentation of pipeline and modules.
KPI	Complexity of the units, unit size, number of classes, structures.
Methods of collection/ measurement and verification/ validation	Analysis of the software code, analysis of the hardware documentation. Analysis of the code and hardware.
Target Value	Maximum number of classes and pipeline modules (e.g., less than 100 classes, pipeline with less than 12 modules, presence/ absence of non-documented elements (magic numbers etc).

Table 4.27 Maintainability (Testability)

NFR aspect	**NFR description**
Name	Characteristic: **Maintainability** Sub-characteristics: **Testability**
Definition	Degree of effectiveness and efficiency with which test criteria can be established for a system, product or component and tests can be performed to determine whether those criteria have been met.
Description	A system must foresee the possibility to conduct tests of individual modules and functionalities
What is measured	Difficulty to run specific test on the system
KPI	Number of tests that can be run on the system, possibility to test individual modules, availability of test data
Methods of collection/ measurement and verification/ validation	Analysis of the code/hardware. Verification of test procedure for each module
Target Value	The minimum number of tests that can be run on each module. (e.g., each module has one or more test with specific data).

4.3.7 Flexibility

Table 4.28 Flexibility (Adaptability)

NFR aspect	**NFR description**
Name	Characteristics: **Flexibility** Sub-Characteristics: **Adaptability**
Definition	Degree to which a system or product can effectively/efficiently be adapted for different or evolving HW/SW or other operational/usage environments.
Description	Adaptability to the evolving AI-based algorithms running on the HW/SW architecture.
What is measured	Types of AI-based algorithms running on the platform.
KPI	Qualitative [Times].
Methods of collection/ measurement and verification/ validation	Demonstrator evaluation. Validation of the types of AI-based algorithms running on the intelligent gateway.
Target Value	The increased number of AI-based algorithms that can be run on the platform in the end of the project compared to the start of the project (e.g., types of AI-based algorithms increased with 3 times from the start to the end of the project).

Table 4.29 Flexibility (Installability)

NFR aspect	**NFR description**
Name	Characteristic: **Flexibility** Sub-characteristics: **Installability**
Definition	Degree of effectiveness and efficiency with which a product or system can be successfully installed and/or uninstalled in a specified environment.
Description	Developed system consisting of software and hardware should be easily deployed and installed in new unknown environments
What is measured	Test on possibility to install the edge device – HW/SW system
KPI	Number of successful installability test as percentage over all tests
Methods of collection/ measurement and verification/ validation	Following procedures in installation/deployment document. Tests of installation in various environments.
Target Value	Number of successful installation tests as percentage [%] versus all tests. (e.g., $>$ 95 % of successful installations).

Table 4.30 Flexibility (Replaceability)

NFR aspect	**NFR description**
Name	Characteristic: **Flexibility** Sub-characteristics: **Replaceability**
Definition	Degree to which a product can replace another specified software product for the same purpose in the same environment.
Description	Testing the capability of one software component to be replaced by another software component within a single system. The system, in regard to the replaced component, should produce the same results that it produced before the replacement.
What is measured	Capacity of the system to produce the expected behaviour when a component has been replaced by another one
KPI	Successful run of the system providing the expected output on a series of tests after replacement
Methods of collection/ measurement and verification/ validation	Replacement of one module and conduction of full system tests. Tests of system after replacement in a number of test cases.
Target Value	Rate of successful runs (in percentage [%]) after replacing a SW component within a single system (e.g., $>$ 95 % of successful runs after module replacement).

5

Edge AI Functional Requirements

5.1 Definition

The edge AI field has emerged in recent years, and there is no specific standardised definition exclusively for edge AI system functional requirements (FRs) in ISO or IEEE standards. The concept of functional requirements for systems, including those incorporating AI, can be framed within the broader context of requirements engineering and system functionalities described in existing standards. This work aims to apply the principles of systems and software, hardware, AI, and data engineering standards. These requirements would focus on what functions an edge AI system must perform, considering its unique characteristics, such as local data processing, minimal latency, and resource constraints.

In this context, edge AI system functional requirements are specifications of what an edge AI system is supposed to do, describing the functions or tasks that the edge AI system must perform to meet its designated operations or to fulfil the needs of its users. These requirements define the behaviours, operations, and processes an edge AI system must execute to satisfy its intended purposes.

Functional requirements are crucial in edge AI systems, which combine hardware, software, AI components, and data development. They clearly describe what needs to be built and serve as a foundation for the edge AI system verification, validation, testing and benchmarking. They typically include inputs, expected outcomes, data handling, processing logic, and interactions with other systems.

Functional requirements describe what an edge AI system, application, or product must do to fulfil its intended purpose. They detail the edge AI system's specific behaviours, functions, and interactions under various

DOI: 10.1201/9788743809586-5

conditions. Functional requirements guide the development process and ensure the final edge AI system (product, algorithm, model) meets user needs and business objectives.

Defining FRs for edge AI systems presents a challenge to traditional RE practices. Classical FRs describe deterministic system behaviours that can be precisely specified and verified. However, the core of edge AI systems is ML and DL models whose behaviour is inherently probabilistic and emergent from the data on which it was trained. It is therefore impossible to specify its exact internal logic or guarantee its correctness on all possible inputs. In the case of edge AI systems, the FRs need to address the observable, verifiable interactions of the system that surrounds it, while the edge AI model is treated as a component with a well-defined interface that provides probabilistic outputs, and the FRs specify the deterministic logic that consumes these outputs.

The ISO/IEC/IEEE 29148:2018 [56] standard defines functional/performance requirements as those that describe the system or system element functions or tasks to be performed by the system. Performance is an attribute of function. A performance requirement alone is an incomplete requirement. Performance is normally expressed quantitatively. There can be more than one performance requirement associated with a single function, functional requirement, or task.

A key technique for structuring these requirements is functional decomposition. This method involves breaking down a high-level user need or system capability into a hierarchy of smaller, more detailed, and independently testable functions. For a typical edge AI system, this decomposition follows the flow of data through the system. For example, a high-level function like requiring the detection and response to anomalies can be decomposed into a verifiable sequence of lower-level functions. This sequence can include that the system acquires data from a specific sensor at a defined frequency and resolution; the system applies a specified filter and normalisation algorithm to the raw data; the system passes the pre-processed data to the AI model for inference; the system receives a classification and a confidence score from the model; if the classification is an anomaly and the confidence score is above a specified threshold, the system executes a defined action, such as activating an alarm or sending a notification; and the system logs all inputs, model outputs, and system actions to a specified memory location.

While the specific functions are domain-dependent, it is possible to define a set of domain-agnostic functional building blocks that are common to most edge AI systems. These include an intelligent data pipeline for ingestion and preprocessing, a scalable engine for model training or inference, a module for model deployment and management, and a mechanism for monitoring and feedback. Structuring FRs around these verifiable building blocks allows engineers to specify and test the edge AI system's behaviour rigorously, even when the AI component itself is probabilistic. This approach makes the system's overall function testable, even if the edge AI's reasoning is not.

When creating edge AI functional requirements, it is vital to remember that they should be specific, measurable, achievable, relevant, and time-bound (SMART). By following these guidelines, developers can be sure that the functional requirements are precise and will help edge AI development build the right system.

When defining the edge AI functional requirements, the designers must describe the KPIs and quantitative and qualitative target measures that are verifiable and follow the SMART criteria. Several considerations should be followed when describing edge AI functional requirements, such as being clearly and precisely described to avoid ambiguity and misunderstandings, feasible considering the technological, time, and resource constraints of the system, written in a way that they can be verified through testing or demonstration and relevant to the users' needs and align with the overall objectives of the edge AI system being developed.

Using the information provided in [45] functional requirements for edge AI systems are specifying what the item should do, aligning to the functional suitability quality characteristic outlined in ISO/IEC 25010:2023 System and software quality models.

5.2 Edge AI Functional Requirements, Key KPIs and Measures.

The following section provides examples (structured in tables) of edge AI functional requirements, KPIs, and measures that researchers and practitioners can use as references for their projects. The performances are related to AI algorithms, data quality, data collection, sensors, communication, system latency, processing time, accuracy, resolution, optimisation, etc.

5.2.1 AI Algorithms

Table 5.1 AI algorithms (Prediction algorithms)

FR aspect	FR description
Name	**AI algorithms**
Definition	Prediction algorithms for energy optimisation at deep-edge.
Description	The ability to take advantage of collected data and optimise energy consumption (residential/office) in a specific period.
What is measured	The optimised energy consumption compared with the actual/measured energy consumption.
KPI	Quantitative [%].
Methods of collection/ measurement and verification/validation	Demonstrator evaluation. Accuracy.
Target Value	Accuracy (in percentage [%]) of AI predicted energy consumption versus actual/measured energy consumption. (e.g., AI model accuracy $\geq$ 90 % for a specified period of time).

Table 5.2 AI algorithms (Pattern recognition, multi-sensor data)

FR aspect	FR description
Name	**AI algorithms**
Definition	AI pattern recognition learning algorithms based on multi-sensor data input.
Description	Pattern recognition capabilities - AI algorithms identifying lighting and environmental characteristics and process adjustment parameters based on sensor data analysis.
What is measured	Recognise.
KPI	Qualitative.
Methods of collection/ measurement and verification/validation	Measure ambient light intensity, ambient light colour components and air quality. Process adjustments to light and share data with BAS/HVAC. Performance.
Target Value	Improvement (in percentage [%]) of light conditions in a building/room based on developed/implemented AI algorithms in the end of the project compared to the start of the project (e.g., 40 % improvement in AI algorithm performance compared to the beginning of the implementation).

Table 5.3 AI algorithms (Pattern recognition, camera data)

FR aspect	FR description
Name	**AI algorithms**
Definition	AI pattern recognition learning algorithms based on RGB Camera data input in natural environment.
Description	Pattern recognition capabilities – AI algorithms identifying grapes in a 2D RGB image.
What is measured	Measure the effective estimated patterns count.
KPI	Pattern recognition algorithms.
Methods of collection/ measurement and verification/ validation	Use of edge device on the autonomous system during the relevant growth period. Strict and manageable manual patterns counting. Comparison with AI estimated counting.
Target value	Yield estimation deviation (in percentage [%]) based on pattern recognition algorithms compared with actual yield (e.g., estimate yield with an error estimation less than 15 %).

5.2.2 Perception

Table 5.4 Perception (Quality)

FR aspect	FR description
Name	**Improved perception**
Definition	Perception is the ability of a robot to perceive and understand its environment
Description	Increase in perception quality in deployment area measured with relevant metric
What is measured	Quality of human action classification
KPI	Mean average-precision (MAP)
Methods of collection/ measurement and verification/validation	Academic benchmark data. Standard generalization tests on out-of-distribution data.
Target Value	Increase in precision compared to state-of-the-art on edge devices. (e.g., +25 increase in mIoU (mean intersection over union) with respect to state-of-the-art on edge devices).

Table 5.5 Perception (Frames per second)

FR aspect	**FR description**
Name	**Improved perception**
Definition	Perception is the ability of a robot to perceive and understand its environment.
Description	Allow more capable models to run on edge hardware by reducing the computational load of foundation models.
What is measured	Frames per second on edge device (FPS).
KPI	Frames per second on edge device.
Methods of collection/ measurement and verification/validation	Academic benchmark data. Standard generalization tests on out-of-distribution data.
Target Value	Achieved percentage increase in frames per second (FPS) (e.g., + 50 % increase in FPS).

5.2.3 Object Detection

Table 5.6 Object detection (Precision)

FR aspect	**FR description**
Name	**Object detection precision**
Definition	In a vision-based object detection algorithm (e.g. traffic sign detection), the system is expected to positively classify as object only the objects of a certain class). The precision measures the ratio between the number of correctly classified positives and the total number of positive detections.
Description	A high precision indicates that the system produces reliable positive detections.
What is measured	Correctly classified positives / total classified positive.
KPI	Precision.
Methods of collection/ measurement and verification/ validation	Test run with benchmark of images.
Target Value	Precision in percentage [%] (e.g., precision > 95 %).

Table 5.7 Object detection (Recall)

FR aspect	FR description
Name	**Object detection recall**
Definition	In a vision-based object detection algorithm (e.g. traffic sign detection), the system is expected to detect all objects of a certain class visible in an input image). The recall measures the ratio between the number of correctly classified positives and the total number of objects of the specified class.
Description	A high recall indicates that the system reliably finds all objects of the given class.
What is measured	Correctly classified positives / total actual positive.
KPI	Recall.
Methods of collection/ measurement and verification/validation	Test run with benchmark of images.
Target Value	Recall in percentage [%] (e.g., recall > 90 %).

5.2.4 Wireless Communication

Table 5.8 Wireless communication (Multiprotocol)

FR aspect	FR description
Name	**Communication multiprotocol.**
Definition	Seamless integration of wireless communication protocols into AI enhanced gateway.
Description	Wireless communication protocols supported and used by the system.
What is measured	Number of compatible wireless protocols used.
KPI	Quantitative [#].
Methods of collection/ measurement and verification/validation	Demonstrator evaluation. Validation of wireless protocols.
Target Value	Number of different wireless protocols supported by the AI enhanced gateway and its system (e.g., at least 3 different wireless protocols).

Table 5.9 Wireless communication (Range)

FR aspect	**FR description**
Name	**Wireless range.**
Definition	Wireless coverage area of the communication protocols integrated in the intelligent gateway.
Description	Wireless communication range optimised for indoors use in a typical residential/office building including normal obstacles.
What is measured	The maximum functional distance between the gateway and nodes/sensors.
KPI	Quantitative [m].
Methods of collection/ measurement and verification/validation	Demonstrator evaluation. Validation of wireless transmission link.
Target Value	Wireless transmission range [m] indoors. (E.g., minimum 30 m inside for at least one communication protocol).

Table 5.10 Wireless communication (Performance)

FR aspect	**FR description**
Name	**Wireless connectivity range.**
Definition	Wireless connectivity with different protocols for lighting nodes for indoor and outdoor usage, gaining reliable data routes and long range.
Description	Wireless protocols supported by the system.
What is measured	Typical node to node range for indoor and outdoor usage.
KPI	Quantitative [#].
Methods of collection/ measurement and verification/validation	Demonstrator evaluation: MESH protocols used in intelligent lighting solutions. Verification and validation of indoor distances above a defined range (e.g., > 50 m indoors).
Target Value	Better performance than "comparable" commercial standards at defined distances (e.g., perform better than commercial standards like Zigbee).

5.2.5 Real-Time

Table 5.11 Real-time functioning (System latency)

FR aspect	FR description
Name	**Real-time functioning**
Definition	To enable real-time use and dynamic learning by minimising time and resource requirements.
Description	Near real-time operation is important for overall user experience and usability of the integrated system.
What is measured	Inference time, end-to-end latency of the system.
KPI	System Latency.
Methods of collection/ measurement and verification/validation	Live Demonstration.
Target Value	Low system latency (near real-time operation if required by the functionality) (e.g., dependent on each functionality (2-60 sec)).

Table 5.12 Video processing real time (Frame processing time)

FR aspect	FR description
Name	**Video processing real-time**
Definition	In a vision-based AI system, input data often comes in form of a video stream with a certain frequency (e.g. 25 frames per second or fps). The system is said to be "video-real-time" if it can process each frame before the next frame arrives in the input.
Description	The video speed induces an available time budget for each frame inversely proportional to the frame rate. The system is said video real time if the processing time of one frame does not exceed the available time budget for each frame.
What is measured	Time necessary to process one frame.
KPI	Proportion of the time budget used to process one frame.
Methods of collection/ measurement and verification/validation	Test run with benchmark of video input.
Target Value	One frame process time versus time budget versus in percentage [%] (e.g., proportion of time budget < 100 %).

5.2.6 Multi-Sensor

Table 5.13 Multi-sensor measurements (Parameters supported)

FR aspect	FR description
Name	**Multi-sensor measurement parameters collection.**
Definition	Realtime multi-sensor data collection in industrial environment with edge computing capabilities.
Description	Type of different sensor measurement parameters supported by the system, (ambient light colour, Environmental data gas content of air, IR occupancy).
What is measured	Number of different parameters monitored/ collected.
KPI	Quantitative [#].
Methods of collection/ measurement and verification/validation	Demonstrator evaluation: monitor ambient light, occupancy and air quality. Data collection from sensors measuring each different parameter.
Target Value	An increased number of different sensor measurement parameters supported compared to baseline/starting point (e.g., > 2 different types of sensor parameters).

5.2.7 Data Completeness

Table 5.14 Data completeness (Data handling layer)

FR aspect	FR description
Name	**Data completeness**
Definition	Degree to which the data in the Data Handling Layer is complete.
Description	Limited availability of data sources, as well as flaws in the setup of the data pipeline could lead to missing data entries in the Data Handling Layer. This could, in turn, negatively impact prediction accuracy.
What is measured	Percentage of empty/nan value in the Data Handling Layer.
KPI	Data completeness.
Methods of collection/ measurement and verification/validation	Data analysis.
Target Value	Increased data completeness [%] compared to baseline/starting point (e.g., 85 %).

5.2.8 Accuracy

Table 5.15 Accuracy (Event detection)

FR aspect	FR description
Name	**Accuracy**
Definition	Event detection accuracy.
Description	Event detection on difficult data lead to failures in detections. We aim at maximizing the number of correct predictions.
What is measured	The accuracy of the events detection and classification.
KPI	Accuracy.
Methods of collection/ measurement and verification/validation	Inference in real-use conditions and careful labelling. Accuracy measurement on various scenes and conditions.
Target Value	Increased accuracy [%] compared to baseline/starting point (e.g., 80 % accuracy).

Table 5.16 Accuracy (Pose estimation)

FR aspect	FR description
Name	**Accuracy of pose estimation algorithms**
Definition	Vision-based pose estimation algorithms take an image or a video sequence as an input and outputs the camera pose (6DoF, rotation and translation w.r.t. to a global coordinate frame). The pose estimated as an output should be as near as possible to the ground truth one.
Description	Pose accuracy can be measured in terms of position estimate (deviation from the Euclidean position) and rotation estimation (deviation from the orientation of the camera).
What is measured	Translation deviation in cm, rotation deviation as a quaternion or Euler angles.
KPI	Mean square error in translation over a sequence, Mean angular error in rotation over a sequence.
Methods of collection/ measurement and verification/validation	Test run with benchmark of video input.
Target Value	Decreased error compared to baseline/starting point (e.g., translation error $<$ 5cm, angular error $<$ 5 degrees).

Table 5.17 Accuracy drop (Network reduction)

FR aspect	**FR description**
Name	**Drop of accuracy after network size reduction**
Definition	When running AI algorithms on an edge device, the neural networks can be trained on a cloud, then reduced in size to fit in the hardware limitation of the edge device. This reduction can be achieved with quantization and pruning techniques but generally leads to a drop of accuracy compared to the vanilla cloud-trained version.
Description	This requirement defines the acceptable loss of accuracy after the network size has been reduced.
What is measured	Performance (depending on the task: accuracy, precision, recall, similarity etc) in the edge version of the algorithm vs original performance.
KPI	Performance drop.
Methods of collection/ measurement and verification/validation	Test run with benchmark of image input.
Target Value	Acceptable performance drop [%] versus network reduction (e.g., acceptable performance drop of 5 %).

5.2.9 Resolution

Table 5.18 Resolution (Images)

FR aspect	**FR description**
Name	**Resolution of input images**
Definition	Edge AI algorithms have limited resources and are able to process images only up to a certain size or resolution. In the case where the input resolution is variable, this functional requirement specifies what is the maximum resolution that the system should be able to process.
Description	Highest image resolution that the system can process.
What is measured	Correct behaviour of the system with a certain resolution image.
KPI	Max image size.
Methods of collection/ measurement and verification/validation	Test run with benchmark of image input.
Target Value	Increased maximum image resolution while maintain correct behaviour compared to baseline/starting point (e.g., size up to 1024 x 1024 pixels).

5.2.10 Optimisation

Table 5.19 Optimisation (Various neural networks)

FR aspect	FR description
Name	**Extensibility of the optimization to various types of Neural Networks**
Definition	The optimization shall be extensible to allow the optimization to be applicable to various types of Neural Networks.
Description	The optimization algorithm shall be extensible to support various types of Neural Networks, including: CNNs, LSTMs and Transformer models.
What is measured	The ability of the optimization algorithm to optimise various types of Neural Network architectures.
KPI	Achieved / Not achieved [Qualitative].
Methods of collection/ measurement and verification/validation	Optimization runs applied to the specified types of Neural Networks. Results showing optimised models for the above specified types of Neural Networks.
Target Value	Shown applicability of the optimization to the above specified types of Neural Networks.

Table 5.20 Optimisation (Neural networks and secondary hardware)

FR aspect	FR description
Name	**Multi-objective Optimization**
Definition	The method/techniques shall concurrently optimise a NN for a reference application to improve the accuracy of predictions while improving a secondary HW-related metric on the target platform.
Description	The multi-objective optimization shall automatically design a CNN for a reference application to achieve high accuracy and low latency on the target inferencing platform.
What is measured	Model task performance and secondary HW-related metric.
KPI	[%] Task Performance and Secondary Metric.
Methods of collection/ measurement and verification/validation	The task performance of the optimised network will be measured on the dataset used to optimise the NN and benchmarked with comparable SOTA networks. The secondary HW-related metric of the network will be measured on the target platform. Dataset performance and HW-related metric measured on the target platform.
Target Value	A task performance increase and secondary HW-related metric improvement over comparable SOTA networks

Table 5.21 Optimisation objectives (Extendibility)

FR aspect	**FR description**
Name	**Extendibility of the optimization objectives**
Definition	The optimization shall be extendable to support the introduction of additional/alternative optimization objectives.
Description	The algorithm shall support the introduction of additional/alternative objectives in addition to accuracy and latency to accommodate diverse customer interests (e.g., memory).
What is measured	Extendibility of the optimization objectives.
KPI	Achieved / Not achieved [Qualitative].
Methods of collection/ measurement and verification/validation	Additional optimization runs will be performed with alternative/additional objectives to prove the extendibility of the algorithm implementation. Model optimised for additional/alternative objectives.
Target Value	Extendible algorithm to accommodate additional/alternative optimization objectives.

Table 5.22 Photometric optimisation (Image generation)

FR aspect	**FR description**
Name	**Similarity of generated images**
Definition	Machine-learning based image generation algorithms such as e.g. face reenactment produces synthetic images that aim to look like realistic versions of the scene. The similarity measures indicate the photometric similarity between a produced images and the ground truth.
Description	When ground truth is available for test benchmark, the photometric similarity can be measured using mean-square-error (MSE) or peak signal-to-noise ratio (PSNR) between images.
What is measured	The MSE represents the cumulative squared error between the generated and the original image, whereas PSNR represents a measure of the peak error. The lower the value of MSE, the lower the error.
KPI	Mean square error or peak signal-to-noise ration.
Methods of collection/ measurement and verification/validation	Test run with benchmark of image input.
Target Value	Increased PSNR [dB] compared to baseline/starting point (e.g., PSNR $>$ 30dB).

6

Legal Requirements for Design and Development of Edge AI Systems

Edge AI as defined in this book combines AI, IoT and edge computing. By decentralising AI models and algorithms on-device, edge AI can support the emergence of models of AI deployments that are more privacy-preserving and afford users more control over their data. Edge AI systems are domains of active research. This means that there is, for the moment, limited consensus and standardized approaches. For the purpose of legal analysis, edge AI remains, therefore, an umbrella term capable of encompassing different technologies, design choices, and architectures.

Existing Union laws provide a comprehensive and robust framework for the design and development of edge AI technologies. However, there is, for the moment, limited guidance on their practical implementation by edge AI providers. Indeed, Union laws and their corresponding official guidelines make no mention of "Edge AI". This means that edge AI systems and models are subject to a fragmented legal landscape, predominantly formulated in technologically neutral terms or, in the case of Regulation (EU) 2024/1689 (Artificial Intelligence Act), in the form of general objectives subject to further technical specification.

The following sections provide a first attempt to identify the corpus of laws and legal requirements relevant for providers of edge AI systems focusing on Union laws of general application[1] setting out *design requirements* and *human rights safeguards* for AI systems and models. Legal considerations relating to *lawfulness* are not reviewed in detail in this contribution.

[1] This means that regimes of *lex specialis* are excluded from the scope of analysis. This refers, for example, to legal rules and requirements that apply to certain regulated products such as medical devices, toys, etc.

DOI: 10.1201/9788743809586-6

6.1 General Data Protection Regulation - Regulation (EU) 2016/679

Regulation (EU) 2016/679 ("General Data Protection Regulation") applies whenever personal data is processed, regardless of the means used, and pursues the double objective of protecting natural persons and fundamental rights, while ensuring the free movement of personal data [109][2]. Processing operations involving personal data are subject to basic design principles, rights to be afforded to data subjects and, depending on the risks, certain additional safeguards for fundamental rights and freedoms. Compliance with these legal requirements is the responsibility of the data controller, i.e., the natural or legal person determining the purposes and means of processing[3]. For this purpose, the Regulation establishes obligations ensuring that appropriate technical and organisational measures and required safeguards are in place (see Table 6.1)[4].

The European Data Protection Board ("EDPB") is an essential body for the implementation of data protection laws, empowered to issue guidance on the consistent application of data protection rules in the Union. The EDPB has begun work on data protection aspects of Artificial Intelligence but has not issued official guidelines yet. It has, however, published an Opinion on certain data protection aspects related to the processing of personal data in the context of AI models and a report on the investigations led at European level on ChatGPT [113, 114]. Most of the Board's analysis in these documents focuses on particular technological applications (i.e., chatbots using LLMs, web scraping) and legal issues (i.e., controllers' legitimate interests and secondary uses of personal data).

The Board, however, recalled and specified the design objectives enshrined in the legal concept of "anonymisation" and the principle of privacy by design in the context of AI models. First, the Board clarifies that AI models trained on personal data can be considered to be anonymous only following

---

[2] Personal data is defined under article 4(1) of Regulation (EU) 2016/679 as 'any information relating to an identified or identifiable natural person ('data subject'); an identifiable natural person is one who can be identified, directly or indirectly, in particular by reference to an identifier such as a name, an identification number, location data, an online identifier or to one or more factors specific to the physical, physiological, genetic, mental, economic, cultural or social identity of that natural person'.

[3] As defined in article 4(7) of Regulation (EU) 2016/679.

[4] For the precise formulation of these requirements, see articles 5, 9, 12-22, 25, 32, and 35 of Regulation (EU) 2016/679.

Table 6.1 Concise Overview of the Main Design Requirements Imposed by the General Data Protection Regulation

Data Protection Principles.	**Data Subjects' Rights.**	**Processing Operations Subject to Additional Safeguards.**	**Conrollers' Obligations.**
• Lawfulness, fairness, and transparency. • Purpose limitation. Data minimisation. • Accuracy. • Storage limitation. • Confidentiality and integrity. • Accountability.	• Information to be provided to data subjects. • Right of access. • Right to rectification. • Right to erasure. • Right to restriction of processing. • Right to data portability. • Right to object. • Automated individual decision-making, including profiling.	• Processing of special categories of personal data. • Individual decisions obtained from fully automated processing. • Processing presenting a high risk to individuals' fundamental rights and freedoms.	• Data protection by design and by default. • Security. • Data protection impact assessment.

a strict assessment ascertaining that the likelihood of direct extraction of instances of training data and the likelihood of obtaining such data through queries, using reasonable means, is insignificant for any data subject whose data is part of the training data set. Residual likelihood of identification is to be assessed considering direct access to the model and an evaluation of the appropriateness and effectiveness of the measures ensuring anonymity. This evaluation may consider (i) the model's design, evaluation, testing and resistance to attack as well as its documentation or (ii) any other approaches offering an equivalent level of protection [113][5].

Second, the Board explained some of the implications of the principle of data protection by design identified during the investigations on ChatGPT. The Board recalls that "the principle of data protection by design [. . .] shall be taken into account at the time of the determination of the means for processing and at the time of the processing itself", and provides examples of measures that can be taken (e.g., filtering criteria for data collection and deletion measures, information of data subjects about the collection and accuracy of the processing, modalities to facilitate the exercise of rights, etc.) [114][6].

[5] See pp. 16-19.

[6] See pp. 5-9.

The implications of certain data protection provisions for AI models have not yet been examined in detail by the Board, including the processing of special categories of data, automated-decision making, data protection impact assessment, and a general and systematic analysis of the principle of data protection by design and by default [113][7].

There is, therefore, limited guidance on key data protection aspects of edge AI models and systems, namely their operation in close proximity to data sources and use-cases relying on local decision-making in real-time.

6.2 Artificial Intelligence Act - Regulation (EU) 2024/1689

Regulation (EU) 2024/1689 ("Artificial Intelligence Act") establishes rules for the development, the placing on the market, the putting into service and the use of AI systems[8] in the Union and a particular regime for General Purpose AI ("GPAI") Models,[9] based on the risks they pose to health, safety, and fundamental rights [115].

Besides the prohibited AI practices which must, in all cases, be observed by AI providers,[10] the risk-based approach relies on AI systems' capabilities and intended purposes to modulate the set of requirements that must be

---

[7] As explained on p. 10.

[8] An AI system is understood as 'a *machine-based system* that is designed to operate with *varying levels of autonomy* and that *may exhibit adaptiveness after deployment*, and that *for explicit or implicit objectives*, *infers, from the inputs it receives, how to generate outputs* such as *predictions, content, recommendations or recommendations* that *can influence physical or virtual environments*' (emphasis added on the seven criteria of the legal definition). See art. 3(1) of Regulation (EU) 2024/1689. On the seven criteria see the development below.

[9] A general-purpose AI model is defined in article 3(63) of Regulation (EU) 2024/1689 as 'an AI model, including where such an AI model is trained with a large amount of data using self-supervision at scale, that displays significant generality and is capable of competently performing a wide range of distinct tasks regardless of the way the model is placed on the market and that can be integrated into a variety of downstream systems or applications, except AI models that are used for research, development or prototyping activities before they are placed on the market'.

[10] The prohibited practices are not reviewed in detail herein. These refer to the placing on the market, the putting into service and use of AI systems that are deemed to pose unacceptable risks by the legislator, including AI enabled manipulation and exploitation, social scoring, individual risk assessment and prediction of criminal offences, untargeted scraping of facial images, biometric categorization for certain 'sensitive' characteristics, and the use of real-time remote biometric identification systems for law enforcement purposes, emotion recognition. Note that AI practices prohibited under other Union laws also apply. See article 5 of Regulation (EU) 2024/1689.

implemented by AI providers[11]. For that purpose, the Act sets out classification rules to identify high-risk AI systems and GPAI models with systemic risks and designates AI systems presenting specific transparency risks. This means that the Act establishes distinct legal requirements for high-risk AI systems, AI systems interacting with individuals or generating content, GPAI models and GPAI models posing systemic risks (See Table 6.2)[12]. The Act also foresees the possibility for providers of low-risk AI systems to comply with all or parts of the requirements applicable to high-risk AI systems on a voluntary basis.

Table 6.2 Concise overview of the main design requirements imposed by the Artificial Intelligence Act

High-risk AI systems.	**Transparency requirements for AI systems interacting with individuals or generating content.**	**GPAI models.**	**GPAI models posing systemic risks.**
• Risk management system. • Data and data governance. • Technical documentation. • Record keeping. • Transparency. • Human oversight. • Accuracy, robustness and cybersecurity. • Quality management system.	• Provision of information to natural persons interacting with the AI system. • Marking in a machine-readable format and detectability of the system's output as artificially generated or manipulated.	• Technical documentation. • No other specific technical requirement.	• Technical documentation. • Model evaluation following state-of-the-art standardized protocols and tools, including adversarial testing of the model. • Mitigation of possible systemic risks stemming from the development, the placing on the market or the use of the model. • Tracking, documentation and reporting of serious incidents and possible corrective measures. • Adequate level of cybersecurity protection for the model and its physical infrastructure.

[11] Other risk categories are delineated in articles 6, 50, 51, 95 and Annex III and XIII of Regulation (EU) 2024/1689.

[12] For the precise formulation of these requirements, see articles 9-15, 17, 50, 53, and 55 of Regulation (EU) 2024/1689.

The Artificial Intelligence Act's implementation is, at the time of writing, still ongoing[13]. The European Commission recently published official guidelines on the definition of AI systems and prohibited AI practices [117, 118]. On the legal definition of "AI systems", the Commission has clarified that it "should not be applied mechanically" and, instead, consider the specific characteristics of each system. This assessment must, therefore, examine all the criteria set out in the definition and ascertain whether the considered system display these elements at the pre-deployment or the post-deployment phases, without the need to demonstrate that they persist across both phases. The criteria of adaptiveness (i.e., self-learning capabilities) is, however, "facultative and thus not a decisive condition for determining whether the system qualifies as an AI system" [117][14].

The Commission also provided clarifications on systems falling outside the scope of the definition. This concerns systems that "have the capacity to infer in a narrow manner" but have "limited capacity to analyse patterns and adjust autonomously their outputs". This refers to (i) systems for improving mathematical optimization, (ii) basic data processing, (iii) systems based on classical heuristics, and (iv) simple prediction systems [117][15].

Future implementation efforts by the European Commission include the development of guidelines on the requirements applicable to high-risk AI systems and transparency obligations for certain AI systems. Other ongoing initiatives for the implementation of the Act include (i) the development of harmonised standards addressing the requirements applicable to high-risk AI systems by CEN-CENELEC [119], and (ii) the development by the AI Office of a code of practice for providers of GPAI models and GPAI models with systemic risk [120][16].

The Artificial Intelligence Act sets out a general framework for AI systems and GPAI models and leaves its technical implementation to AI providers. In turn, the text does not address the specificities of edge AI

[13] The AIA will apply from 2 August 2026, with particular timelines for the application of certain provisions including, for example, prohibited AI practices which are in force since the 2 February 2025, General-Purpose AI Models (2 August 2025), and high-risk AI systems (2 August 2027).

[14] On pp. 1, 2, and 4.

[15] On pp. 8-10.

[16] Both initiatives are, at the time of writing, still ongoing and therefore not detailed here. On CEN-CENELEC's mandate, see the developments on pp. 113 et sq. below. The final version of the code of practice for GPAI models was published on 10 July 2025 and has yet to be assessed by Member States and the Commission. It is available at <https://digital-strategy.ec.europa.eu/en/policies/contents-code-gpai>.

systems and models in detail. This means that several legal assessments must be carried out on a case-by-case basis, including (i) the applicability of both the Act and the definitions of AI systems and GPAI models, and (ii) an assessment of the intended purpose of edge AI systems and the capabilities of GPAI models deployed at the edge for the purpose of ascertaining applicable risk classifications and requirements. Further reflection on the implementation of the Act's requirements is needed, considering the specificities of edge AI systems, such as their decentralized architectures, proximity to data sources and real-time decision making, as well as the use of local data for training purposes.

6.3 Data Act - Regulation (EU) 2023/2854

Regulation (EU) 2023/2854 ("Data Act") will set rules on access to certain IoT data and the sharing of private sector data and will define technical and organisational requirements for these operations in Business-to-Consumer ("B2C") and Business-to-Business ("B2B") contexts [121][17]. In particular, the regulation will secure and provide a framework for the exercise of user rights to access and share their data on the performance, use and environment of connected products and related services[18].

Users of connected products must be able to access their data, either directly from the connected product or indirectly by a simple request to the data holder. Users are also entitled to request from the data holder the sharing of their data to a third party of their choice, provided that the recipient does not qualify as a "gatekeeper"[19]. For these purposes, the Data Act defines the manner in which the data must be made available to users and data recipients,

---

[17] This refers to Chapter II and III of the Data Act. Other chapters and provisions are not examined in detail, including the conditions for data sharing in Business-to-Government ('B2G') contexts.

[18] This refers to 'product data' and 'related service data' defined, respectively, in articles 2(15) and 2(16) of Regulation (EU) 2023/2854 as 'data generated by the use of a connected product that the manufacturer designed to be retrievable, via an electronic communications service, physical connection or on-device access, by a user, data holder or a third party, including, where relevant, the manufacturer' and 'data representing the digitisation of user actions or of events related to the connected product, recorded intentionally by the user or generated as a by-product of the user's action during the provision of a related service by the provider'.

[19] A 'gatekeeper' is defined as an 'undertaking providing core platform services' that has a significant market impact, provides a core platform service enabling business users to reach end users, and enjoys an entrenched and durable market position. Gatekeepers are designated

Table 6.3 Concise overview of the main requirements relating to data access and sharing imposed by the Data Act

Accessibility	Format and Quality
• User access by design and by default and, where technically feasible, directly from the connected product. • User and data recipient access must be provided in an easy and secure manner, and free of charge. • The data holder must make data accessible to the user or data recipient without undue delay and, where relevant and technically feasible, in a continuous manner and in real-time.	• Users and data recipients must receive product data and related service data or readily available data, as well as the metadata relevant for their interpretation and use. • The data must be made available in a comprehensive, structured, commonly used, and machinereadable format. • Where the data is accessed from the data holder, it must be of the same quality as is available to the data holder.

as well as requirements on data quality and format that apply regardless of the party concerned (i.e., user and data recipient) and the type of user access (i.e., direct or indirect) (see Table 6.3)[20].

The Data Act entered into force on 11 January 2024 and will become applicable on 12 September 2025[21]. It is important to note that the user, in the sense of the Data Act, is not necessarily the data subject. Where such is the case, the data holder and the data recipients must comply with data protection laws. The data holder is, furthermore, subject to the safeguards of the ePrivacy Directive when applicable [121][22]. Further reflexion on the application of the Data Act and its relation to the abovementioned Union laws could be useful for manufacturers and users of edge AI systems.

6.4 Cyber Resilience Act - Regulation (EU) 2024/2847

Regulation (EU) 2024/2847 ("Cyber Resilience Act") imposes horizontal cybersecurity requirements for all products with digital elements made available on the market [123][23]. The concept of products with digital elements[24]

---

by the European Commission and include, at the time of writing, Alphabet, Amazon, Apple, ByteDance, Meta, and Microsoft [122].

[20] For the precise formulation of these requirements, see articles 3(1), 4(1), 5(1), 5(3) and 11 of Regulation (EU) 2023/2854.

[21] Note that the Act foresees a particular timeline for certain products, services, and contracts.

[22] As stated in articles 4(12), 5(7), and 6(1) of Regulation (EU) 2023/2854.

[23] For a detailed review of the Cyber Resilience Act, see [124].

[24] A product with digital elements is defined under article 3(1) of Regulation (EU) 2024/2847 as 'a software or hardware product and its remote data processing solutions, including software or hardware components being placed on the market separately'.

includes AI systems regardless of the risks they pose. Product manufacturers will be responsible for the implementation of security requirements as well as vulnerability handling processes that remain effective throughout products support period (Table 6.4)[25]. The implementation of these requirements is subject to a cybersecurity risk assessment which, for AI systems, shall additionally examine risks and vulnerabilities specific to AI systems.

Table 6.4 Concise overview of the essential cybersecurity requirements imposed by the Cyber Resilience Act

Security requirements	Vulnerability handling requirements
• Design, development and production of products with digital elements in a way that ensures an appropriate level of cybersecurity based on the risks. • Absence of known exploitable vulnerabilities. • Secure by default configuration. • Security updates addressing vulnerabilities and corresponding user controls and settings. • Protection from unauthorised access by appropriate control mechanisms. • Protection of the confidentiality of the processed data. • Protection of the integrity of the processed data. • Data minimisation. • Protection of the availability of essential and basic functions, also after an incident. • Minimisation of the negative impact on the availability of services provided by other devices or networks. • Reduction of the impact of incidents through design, development and production measures. • Provision of security related information to the user. • User controls enabling the secure and permanent removal of all data and settings and, where applicable, their secure portability to other products or systems.	• Identification and documentation of vulnerabilities and components contained in products. • Addressing and remediating vulnerabilities without delay. • Application of effective and regular tests and reviews of the productâĂŹs security. • Sharing and public disclosure of information on fixed vulnerabilities. • Implementation and enforcement of a policy on coordinated vulnerability disclosure. • Measures facilitating the sharing of information about potential vulnerabilities in products and third-party components contained therein. • Mechanisms for the secure distribution of updates. • Requirements on the dissemination of security updates.

The Cyber Resilience Act entered into force on 10 December 2024 but is not yet applicable[26] and, for this reason, no guidance has been issued by the European Commission at the time of writing. The Commission will have the

[25] For the precise formulation of these requirements, see articles 6, 13 and Annex I of Regulation (EU) 2024/2847.

[26] The Act will apply from 11 December 2027, except for manufacturers' reporting obligations concerning actively exploited vulnerabilities and severe incidents having an impact on products' security to Computer Security Incident Responses Teams designated as coordinator

opportunity to provide guidance to manufacturers subject to the simultaneous application of the Cyber Resilience Act and other Union legislation. In that regard, guidance on the interplay between this Act and the Artificial Intelligence Act could be useful also for manufacturers of edge AI systems.

at national level and the European Union Agency for Cybersecurity through the future single reporting platform.

7

Standards

7.1 AI Standards

AI standardisation activities are receiving attention across various Standard Development Organizations (SDOs) to address the diverse challenges and opportunities AI technologies present. These SDOs include international bodies such as ISO, IEC, IEEE, and regional organisations like ETSI and CEN-CENELEC.

ISO and IEC are collaborating on a joint technical committee (JTC 1) that focuses on standardising AI across different dimensions, such as terminology, risk management, and ethical considerations. This committee has initiated the development of standards that outline best practices for AI implementation, ensuring interoperability, safety, and reliability in AI systems. Their work also emphasises the importance of transparency and accountability, with an aim to facilitate trust in AI technologies among users and stakeholders.

The IEEE has established its Global Initiative 2.0 on Ethics of Autonomous and Intelligent Systems, striving to lead standardisation activities that promote ethical considerations and inclusive practices in AI development. Through initiatives like the IEEE 7010 series [63], which focuses on the ethical considerations of autonomous systems, IEEE addresses challenges specific to AI, such as real-time processing, and the safe deployment of AI algorithms in edge environments. These standards emphasise the importance of reliability and resilience in AI applications.

IEEE's efforts focus on creating standards that guide technical aspects and encompass values such as fairness, accountability, and privacy. Their extensive engagement with industry stakeholders, academia, and policymakers aims to address the societal impacts of AI technologies and ensure that standards reflect diverse perspectives.

ETSI is also actively involved in AI standardisation, particularly in relation to telecommunications and the IoT. It is working on frameworks that facilitate the integration of AI into network and service management while

DOI: 10.1201/9788743809586-7

addressing security and privacy challenges. By providing guidelines and standards, ETSI aims to enhance the deployment of AI-driven solutions within its domains, fostering innovation while ensuring compliance with regulatory requirements.

CEN-CENELEC Joint Technical Committee 21 on "Artificial Intelligence" [169] created a dedicated task group (TG) dedicated to inclusiveness with the aim to elaborate recommendations to ensure and improve the inclusiveness of standards for AI and to contribute to their implementation.

Moreover, OECD has developed principles for AI [82] that focus on promoting AI's beneficial use while addressing its potential risks. These principles serve as a foundation for member countries to consider in their policymaking and standardisation efforts. The OECD AI Principles were initially adopted in 2019 and updated in May 2024.

The digital transformation of industrial sectors is highly dynamic, and standardisation plays an essential role in achieving the objectives set for this transformation. In this context, AI standardisation efforts and industry AI efforts are intertwined. Industrial AI applications rely on standardisation to build and sustain trust in industrial AI. Conversely, standardisation relies on industrial AI applications to play an essential role in forming emerging AI standards. Even though the challenges involved differ from those of similar processes in the consumer market, AI standardisation is a lever for the industry's digitalisation journey [71].

AI standardisation activities across SDOs are multifaceted, addressing technical, ethical, and societal dimensions of AI technologies. The SDOs are working collaboratively to create frameworks and guidelines that ensure AI systems are safe, reliable, transparent, and aligned with ethical principles, thereby laying the groundwork for responsible innovation in the AI landscape.

The evolution of the standardisation landscape itself reveals a significant strategic shift. Early efforts were focused on foundational questions, such as defining a common terminology to answer the question, "What is AI?". However, spurred by widespread deployment and regulatory responses to the risks posed by AI, the focus has pivoted dramatically towards operational governance, seeking to answer the question, "How do we build, manage, and verify trustworthy AI and edge AI systems?". This transition is evident in the work of ISO/IEC, which has progressed from foundational standards like the terminology in ISO/IEC 22989:2022 to comprehensive management system standards like ISO/IEC 42001:2023 [180] Similarly, the work of CEN-CENELEC JTC 21is almost entirely dedicated to operationalising the requirements on health, safety and fundamental rights established by the AI Act [126, 149]. This shift reflects the evolution of the industry itself, extending the activities from technological capability to addressing the accountability and control as well.

In Europe, the relationship between product legislation and European standards is particularly important, a concern reflected in the AIA [116]. The law defines essential requirements for high-risk AI systems and general-purpose AI models which will be subject to further technical specification by ESOs by means of European harmonised standards. The AIA does not merely request standards; it actively shapes their content, scope, and timeline, creating a top-down demand that accelerates their development [9]. This creates a feedback loop where policy defines the high-level objectives, the "what," such as the requirements for managing risk in high-risk systems, and the SDOs define the technical implementation, the "how," such as the specific processes and documentation for a compliant risk management system. This model differs from traditional, bottom-up standardisation and has the specificity of focusing on the development of standards that are linked to legal obligations, making them indispensable for any organisation wishing to operate within the common European market.

As mentioned in this chapter, the standards and standardisation activities address AI technology and applications and are not focusing specific at edge AI. The standardisation of edge AI is still in its early stages and is often intertwined with broader standardisation efforts in AI, the IoT, and telecommunications. The challenges for edge AI include resource constraints, decentralised data governance, and the need for robust and efficient models that can operate with limited connectivity. IEEE has begun to address this space with standards like IEEE 2846-2022 [187] on safety models for automated vehicles, which often rely on edge processing, and IEEE 3652.1-2020 [188] on federated machine learning, a key enabling technology for privacy-preserving edge AI [78]. ETSI's work on securing AI is also highly relevant to the edge, as decentralised systems can present unique security vulnerabilities. As edge AI continues to grow, there will be an increasing need for dedicated standards that address its specific architectural, performance, and security requirements.

While standardisation for general AI is accelerating rapidly, the domain of edge AI presents a more nascent and fragmented picture. Edge AI, which involves deploying AI models and processing data on or near the devices where it is generated, introduces unique challenges related to resource constraints, network latency, security, and distributed management [125].

Standardisation for edge AI is not driven by a single, unified effort but instead is emerging from the convergence of work in telecommunications, industrial automation, and device-level engineering. This overview will systematically dissect the contributions of each major SDO, analyse the domains they cover for both general and edge AI, and provide a synthesised analysis of the synergies, gaps, and future trajectory of this critical field.

As edge AI technology matures and emerges as a critical focus area due to the increasing adoption of decentralised computing models, standardisation activities will address edge AI, focusing on specific factors such as latency, bandwidth limitations, and data privacy.

7.1.1 ISO/IEC: Building the Foundational Layer for AI

The joint efforts of ISO and IEC represent an important development for creating broad, horizontal standards for AI. The work is led by the Joint Technical Committee 1, Subcommittee 42 (ISO/IEC JTC 1/SC 42) [150], which was established in 2018 to serve as the central point for AI standardisation across both organisations. SC 42 employs an ecosystem approach, aiming to develop an integrated and interoperable suite of standards that addresses the entire AI lifecycle, from foundational concepts to governance and trustworthiness. This approach is designed to provide a stable, internationally agreed-upon foundation upon which domain-specific and application-level standards can be built.

7.1.1.1 Foundational Concepts and Frameworks

A central activity of the SC 42 portfolio is establishing a common language and conceptual understanding. ISO/IEC 22989:2022, Information technology - Artificial intelligence - Artificial intelligence concepts and terminology, serves this critical function. It provides authoritative definitions for core concepts such as “AI system,” “machine learning,” and “deep learning,” models creating a universal vocabulary that is essential for ensuring consistency and preventing ambiguity across the entire global landscape of AI standards, and technical literature. An AI system, for instance, is defined as an “engineered system that generates outputs such as content, forecasts, recommendations or decisions for a given set of human-defined objectives” [21]. This foundational work ensures that when different standards or organisations discuss AI, they are operating from a shared set of definitions.

ISO/IEC:2022 [21] states that concepts and categories of AI allow for a comparison and classification of different solutions with respect to properties like trustworthiness, robustness, resilience, reliability, accuracy, safety, security and privacy, while ISO/IEC TR 24028:2020 [43] has as aim to establish trust in AI systems through transparency, explainability, controllability, etc. present the engineering pitfalls and typical associated threats and risks to AI systems, along with possible mitigation techniques and methods; and provide approaches to assess and achieve availability, resiliency, reliability, accuracy, safety, security and privacy of AI systems to ensure responsible use of AI, traceability, transparency and reliability as stated by ISO/IEC 42001:2023 [180].

Building on this terminological base, SC 42 has developed several framework standards that provide a high-level structure for AI development and management. ISO/IEC 23053:2022 [41], "Framework for Artificial Intelligence (AI) Systems Using Machine Learning (ML)", is a key document that describes the end-to-end pipeline for ML-based systems. It outlines the distinct phases of the ML lifecycle, including data acquisition and preparation, model training, verification and validation, model deployment, and ongoing operation and monitoring. This standard provides a crucial architectural reference for organisations building and deploying ML solutions.

To integrate AI development into established engineering practices, ISO/IEC 5338:2023 [135], "Information technology - Artificial intelligence - AI system life cycle processes", adapts the well-known software lifecycle processes from ISO/IEC/IEEE 12207-2017 for the unique needs of AI systems. It incorporates the AI system lifecycle phases defined in ISO/IEC 22989:2022 from inception and design through to retirement-and integrates the ML pipeline from ISO/IEC 23053:2022. It introduces new processes specific to AI, such as a knowledge acquisition process for rule-based systems and an "AI data engineering process" to handle the complexities of preparing datasets for model training. The standards are aligned with system and software engineering lifecycle standards ISO/IEC/IEEE standards [55–59].

7.1.1.2 Management Systems, Risk, and Trustworthiness

Perhaps the most impactful standard from SC 42 is ISO/IEC 42001:2023, "Information technology - Artificial intelligence - Management system". This is an AI Management System (AIMS) standard modelled after other successful management system standards like ISO 9001:2015 [181] (quality) and ISO/IEC 27001:2022 [182] (information security), ISO/IEC 42001:2023 provides a structured, certifiable framework for organisations to govern their development, provision, or use of AI systems responsibly. It offers a systematic approach to managing risks and opportunities related to AI, helping to harmonise innovation with governance and providing a clear path for organisations to demonstrate their commitment to responsible AI practices to regulators, customers, and other stakeholders.

Complementing the AIMS is ISO/IEC 23894:2023 [183], "Information Technology – Artificial Intelligence – Guidance on risk management", which provides specific guidance on implementing risk management for AI systems. The standard adapts the generic principles of ISO 31000:2018 [184] for the unique risks posed by AI, such as algorithmic bias, data quality issues, model drift, and adversarial attacks. It provides methodologies for identifying, assessing, and mitigating these risks throughout the AI system lifecycle, offering a practical framework for both technical and operational risk management.

The concept of trustworthiness is a central theme in SC 42's work, addressed horizontally across multiple documents. ISO/IEC TR 24028:2020, "Information technology – Artificial intelligence - Overview of trustworthiness in artificial intelligence", provides a high-level framework for this concept, breaking it down into constituent components such as reliability, availability, resilience, accountability, safety, security, and privacy. It also introduces key properties like ability, integrity, and benevolence as assessable quality components of trustworthiness.

Specific aspects of trustworthiness are explored in greater detail in dedicated technical reports and standards. ISO/IEC TR 24027:2021 [137], "Information technology – Artificial intelligence - Bias in AI systems and AI aided decision making", provides a comprehensive overview of the sources and types of bias, from human cognitive biases to data-driven and algorithmic biases, and offers methods for their mitigation. The forthcoming ISO/IEC TS 6254:2025 [138], "Information technology - Artificial intelligence - Objectives and approaches for explainability and interpretability of machine learning (ML) models and artificial intelligence (AI) systems" addresses the critical areas of explainability and interpretability of AI systems, providing a taxonomy of explanation needs and methods for assessment.

In this context, the definition of guidelines for the application of data governance and data quality in AI systems is crucial. Addressing bias in the data of technological systems is a significant challenge in the digital age, as the decisions made by algorithms can have substantial societal and personal implications, which can be measured according to the ISO/IEC standards [132].

7.1.1.3 Quality and Data for AI Systems

Recognising that AI systems are fundamentally software-based, SC 42 has worked in close collaboration with ISO/IEC JTC 1/SC 7 (Software and systems engineering) to adapt existing software quality models for AI. The forthcoming ISO/IEC 25059:2023 [136], Quality model for AI-based systems, extends the widely used SQuaRE series (ISO/IEC 25000) [44–52]. It proposes modifications to the standard quality characteristics defined in ISO/IEC 25010:2023 to make them more relevant for AI. For example, it adds "User Controllability" and "Transparency" as sub-characteristics of Usability, and "Robustness" as a sub-characteristic of reliability, reflecting the unique quality demands of intelligent systems.

Data is key for AI and edge AI systems, and its quality is paramount. SC 42 has dedicated a significant effort to standardising data quality specifically for analytics and machine learning. The ISO/IEC 5259 series of standards provide a complete foundation for this topic. This multi-part standard is crucial because it differentiates between the quality of general-purpose data, covered by ISO/IEC 25012:2008, and the specific quality requirements of datasets used for training, validation, and testing ML models. While ISO/IEC 25012:2008 addresses characteristics like accuracy and completeness, the ISO/IEC 5259 series introduce additional, ML-specific characteristics such as "balance," "diversity," "relevance," and "representativeness," which are critical for building fair and effective models. ISO/IEC 5259-2:2024 [141] provides explicit data quality measures for these new characteristics, while other parts cover management requirements and a process framework. ISO/IEC 5339:2024 guides AI applications based on a common framework to provide multiple macro-level perspectives. The framework incorporates "make", "use" and "impact" perspectives. It includes AI characteristics and non-functional characteristics such as trustworthiness and risk management. The guidance can be used by standards developers, application developers, and other interested parties to provide answers to the question: "What are the characteristics and considerations of an AI application?". The stakeholders are mapped to various stages of the AI system life cycle, highlighting their roles and responsibilities and making them aware of the processes to follow to enable a coherent stakeholder engagement for the AI application. These stakeholders can have various levels of AI expertise and knowledge. Since AI applications can differ from non-AI software applications due to their continuously evolving nature and aspects of trustworthiness, all stakeholders should be made aware of AI-specific characteristics [134].

A defining characteristic of SC 42's strategy is the development of a deeply interconnected system of standards rather than a collection of isolated documents. This architectural approach ensures coherence and interoperability across the portfolio. For example, the terminology defined in ISO/IEC 22989:2022 is the common language used throughout all other SC 42 standards, including the AIMS in ISO/IEC 42001:2023. The risk management principles from ISO/IEC 23894:2023 are an integral component of the management system defined in ISO/IEC 42001:2023. Likewise, the data quality requirements from the ISO/IEC 5259 series are essential inputs for the ML framework described in ISO/IEC 23053:2022. This deliberate design creates a holistic and non-contradictory suite of standards that organisations can use together to build and govern complex, trustworthy AI systems from the ground up.

Despite the comprehensive nature of this foundational work, a review of the published and active projects within SC 42 reveals a conspicuous absence of standards explicitly scoped for edge AI. The portfolio focuses almost entirely on horizontal concepts-risk, governance, quality, data-that apply to AI systems regardless of their deployment environment. This implies that, from the perspective of ISO and IEC, edge AI is not considered a fundamentally new technological paradigm requiring its unique foundational standards. Instead, it is viewed as a specific deployment context or application domain. An organisation developing an edge AI system would be expected to apply the existing ISO/IEC standards for risk management, data quality, and governance, just as an organisation developing a cloud-based AI system would. This strategic choice to remain horizontal and foundational creates an opportunity and a clear need for other, more specialised SDOs to develop the practical, implementation-focused standards required for the unique challenges of the edge.

7.1.2 IEEE: A Focus on Ethics and Practical Implementation

The Institute of Electrical and Electronics Engineers (IEEE) has established a distinctive and influential position in the AI standardisation landscape through a dual-focus strategy. At the same time, the IEEE Standards Association (IEEE SA) has become a global leader in developing frameworks to address the ethical and societal dimensions of AI, translating abstract principles into actionable engineering processes. In this context, IEEE SA's technical committees, are developing efficient, engineering-centric standards that address specific implementation challenges, with a notable pioneering role in the domain of edge AI [152].

7.1.2.1 The Ethical Dimension: Codifying Principles in the P7000 Series

The IEEE's most visible contribution to responsible AI is the P7000™ series of standards, a comprehensive portfolio dedicated to "Ethically Aligned Design". The P7000 series represents a concerted effort to systematically embed ethical considerations into the AI system design and development lifecycle. The P7000 series is designed to provide engineers and developers with concrete, actionable processes and guidelines, and effectively bridges the gap between high-level ethical principles and day-to-day engineering practice to ensure that values are built into systems by design, not merely assessed as an afterthought.

The flagship standard of this series is IEEE 7000-2021 [189], "IEEE Standard Model Process for Addressing Ethical Concerns During System Design". It provides a systematic process for identifying and analysing potential ethical issues from the outset of a project, integrating value-based considerations into system requirements and design choices. This is complemented by IEEE 7001-2021 [190], "IEEE Standard for Transparency of Autonomous Systems", which specifies what information about an AI system should be accessible and to whom, providing a framework for clear and understandable disclosures.

Other key standards in the series tackle specific ethical challenges. IEEE 7003-2024 [192], "IEEE Standard for Algorithmic Bias Considerations", guides identifying and mitigating unintended bias in algorithms, a critical issue for fairness and equity.

IEEE 7002-2022 [191], "IEEE Standard Data Privacy Process", defines a process for managing data privacy throughout the system lifecycle, aligning with global privacy principles [109–112]. The series extends to a wide range of societal concerns, with standards addressing the governance of child and student data (IEEE P7004-2020 [193], "Standard for Child and Student Data Governance"), fail-safe design for autonomous systems (IEEE 7009-2024 [195], "IEEE Standard for Fail-Safe Design of Autonomous and Semi-Autonomous Systems"), and even the ethics of AI-driven "nudging" (IEEE P7008-2017 [194], "Standard for Ethically Driven Nudging for Robotic, Intelligent and Autonomous Systems"). To further promote these principles, IEEE SA has also launched certification programs like IEEE CertifAIEd™

to assess the ethics in the creation and implementation of Autonomous Intelligent Systems (AIS).

7.1.2.2 The Practical Dimension: Standardising Edge AI Implementation

While ISO/IEC provides the foundational "what" and "why" of AI governance, IEEE has taken a leading role in defining the practical "how" of edge AI implementation. Recognising the unique engineering challenges of deploying AI on resource-constrained devices, IEEE has initiated several standards projects that provide concrete guidance for developers and system architects [153]. This work fills a critical gap left by the more abstract, horizontal standards from other organisations and is driven by a bottom-up response to immediate engineering needs in the rapidly growing edge AI market.

A landmark project in this area is IEEE P3342-2023 [125], "Standard for Functional Requirements of Toolchain for Artificial Intelligence Model Deployment on Edge Devices". This standard is one of the first of its kind to directly address the end-to-end engineering pipeline required to take a trained AI model and make it run efficiently at the edge. Its scope covers the entire toolchain, specifying functional requirements for crucial steps such as frontend adaptation (converting models from different frameworks), model compression (e.g., quantisation and pruning to reduce size and computational cost), graph optimisation (to streamline model execution), backend adaptation (targeting specific edge hardware), and runtime optimisation. This provides a standardised blueprint for building the software infrastructure needed to operationalise edge AI.

Another key standard is IEEE P2975.3-2023 [154], "Recommended Practice for Software Framework for Industrial Artificial Intelligence (AI) at-the-edge". This project focuses on a key vertical application for edge AI: industrial control systems. It describes a software framework, including key features and software building blocks, for deploying AI at the edge in a manufacturing or industrial context. This is vital for applications like predictive maintenance and process automation, where low latency and high reliability are paramount. By defining functionalities and interfaces, this standard promotes interoperability and simplifies the integration of AI into complex industrial environments [154].

Beyond these specific edge standards, IEEE is also working on related enabling technologies. For example, IEEE P3652.1-2020, "Guide for Architectural Framework and Application of Federated Machine Learning", addresses a key technique for training AI models across distributed devices without centralising sensitive data. This is inherently an edge-centric paradigm that is crucial for privacy-preserving AI in sectors like healthcare and consumer electronics. These practical, engineering-focused standards demonstrate IEEE's focus to provide the tangible tools and frameworks necessary to build and deploy real-world AI and edge AI systems.

7.1.3 ETSI: Standardising AI for the Communications and Edge Ecosystem

The European Telecommunications Standards Institute (ETSI) plays a unique and critical role in the AI standardisation landscape, with a primary focus on enabling AI and edge AI applications [155] through the standardisation of network and communications infrastructure. ETSI's strategy can be understood not as an attempt to standardise AI algorithms or models themselves, but rather to standardise the underlying "plumbing" the network platforms and architectures that allows innovative AI services to be deployed efficiently, securely, and at scale. This network-centric approach is epitomised by its pioneering work in Multi-access Edge Computing (MEC), which has become a foundational technology for the entire edge AI ecosystem.

7.1.3.1 Multi-access Edge Computing (MEC) as the Enabler for Edge AI

ETSI's Industry Specification Group on Multi-access Edge Computing (ISG MEC) was established to create a standardised, open environment that brings cloud-computing capabilities to the edge of the network, typically within the Radio Access Network (RAN) [146]. The MEC architecture is designed to provide an IT service environment characterised by properties that are essential for high-performance edge AI: ultra-low latency, high bandwidth, and real-time access to radio network information that applications can leverage for context-aware operations. By creating this standardised platform, ETSI enables a competitive ecosystem where third-party application developers, including AI service providers, can deploy their services on any compliant operator's network, fostering innovation on top of a stable infrastructure.

The link between MEC and the requirements of edge AI is direct and explicit. ETSI's white paper, "MEC support towards Edge Native Design", details how the MEC platform is purpose-built to address the challenges of running sophisticated AI applications at the edge. Many modern AI models, large language models or high-resolution video analytics models, are too computationally intensive to run on resource-constrained end-user devices like smartphones or IoT sensors. MEC provides the solution by enabling task offloading, where these intensive computational workloads can be moved to a nearby MEC server within the network, achieving low-latency processing without the long round-trip delay of sending data to a distant cloud data centre [157]. This capability is critical for use cases like real-time augmented reality, interactive gaming, V2X communications, and industrial automation.

ETSI has published a comprehensive set of specifications that define the MEC architecture and its interfaces [156–158]. Key standards include ETSI GS MEC 003, which describes the Framework and Reference Architecture, and ETSI GS MEC 011, which specifies Edge Platform Application Enablement. These standards detail how applications are managed, how they discover and consume edge services, and how they interact with the underlying network. This standardised framework is the key to enabling a multi-vendor, multi-operator edge ecosystem where AI applications can be deployed seamlessly.

7.1.3.2 Securing AI and Fostering Network Evolution

Beyond enabling the platform, ETSI is also addressing the security of the AI systems that will run on it. The ETSI Technical Committee on Securing AI (TC SAI) was formed to tackle the novel security vulnerabilities associated with AI systems, such as prompt injection and data poisoning attacks. In a significant development, TC SAI has produced a technical specification on Baseline Cyber Security Requirements for AI Models and Systems [159]. This is reported to be the first global standard that defines a robust set of minimum-security requirements that apply across the entire AI lifecycle, from secure design and development to secure deployment, maintenance, and end-of-life. This provides a crucial security baseline for all stakeholders in the AI supply chain, from model developers to system operators.

The demanding requirements of edge AI applications are not only served by the network but are also a powerful force driving the evolution of the network itself. The need for ultra-low latency and high throughput required by data-intensive AI models is a significant catalyst for the deployment of 5G networks and the continued development of MEC and future 6G architectures. AI is not merely a passive service running on the network; its performance requirements are actively shaping the design and capabilities of next-generation communication systems. This positions AI as a key business driver for telecommunication operators, who can leverage their MEC infrastructure to offer premium, low-latency services for a new generation of intelligent applications.

ETSI's work also extends to fostering data interoperability for AI agents [160]. Recognising that the proliferation of autonomous AI applications will create complex data sharing patterns, ETSI has launched a group to develop technical standards for data and semantic interoperability. This work will address fundamental aspects like data representation, access control, and privacy preservation, initially focusing on telecom networks and later expanding to other sectors like industrial applications and eHealth. Through these multifaceted efforts, ETSI is building the critical network and security infrastructure necessary for a robust and trustworthy edge AI ecosystem.

7.1.4 ITU-T: Integrating AI into Global Telecommunication Networks

ITU-T approaches AI standardisation from the perspective of a global standards body responsible for the interoperability and operation of worldwide telecommunication networks. Its work is primarily focused on how AI can be integrated into the fabric of these networks to improve their efficiency, enable new services, and manage their increasing complexity. This network-centric viewpoint leads to a focus on "AI for networks" (AI4N) and the development of architectures where intelligence is a native component of the network itself [162, 164].

7.1.4.1 From AI for Networks to AI-Native Architectures

The central body for this work within the ITU-T is Study Group 13 (SG13), which serves as the lead study group on "Future networks and emerging network technologies," with a specific mandate covering the application of AI and machine learning in networks. A foundational document from this group is Recommendation ITU-T Y.3172, Architectural framework for machine learning in future networks including IMT-2020. Approved in 2019, this recommendation was one of the first to provide a standardised architecture for embedding ML functions within the network, defining logical components and interfaces for tasks like data collection, model training, and policy-driven network management.

Building on this foundation, the ITU-T's vision has evolved towards the concept of "AI-native" networks. In July 2024, SG13 established a new Focus Group on AI-Native for Telecommunication Networks (FG-AINN)

[162, 163]. This group's objective is to explore the fundamental architectural changes required to move beyond simply applying AI to existing networks and instead to design networks where AI is deeply embedded in the core architecture from the ground up. The goal is to create networks capable of self-management, self-optimisation, and self-repair, enabling unprecedented levels of automation and intelligence to meet the demands of future applications requiring extreme agility and precision [162]. This work represents a paradigm shift, viewing AI not as an add-on tool but as an intrinsic property of the network itself.

This focus on using AI to manage and optimise the network infrastructure is a key differentiator for the ITU-T. Concepts like "autonomous networks" and "AI-native networks" are primarily concerned with making the network more efficient, resilient, and automated for the benefit of the network operator [161]. Use cases being explored by groups like FG-AINN include using large language models for network anomaly resolution and AI-based modelling for network optimisation. This "AI for the network" perspective is distinct from the "AI on the network" perspective of application developers, positioning the network operator as the primary user of the AI technology being standardised.

7.1.4.2 Standardising Intelligent Edge Computing (IEC)

The ITU-T has formally recognised and standardised the convergence of edge computing and artificial intelligence through its work on "Intelligent Edge Computing" (IEC). This work acknowledges that the network edge is not just a location for distributed processing but a critical point of intelligence within the overall network architecture. Recommendation ITU-T Q.5001 [166] defines IEC and specifies its architecture, signalling requirements, and use cases [165]. The standard explicitly states that IEC solves issues like network bottlenecks by "applying the intelligent data processing functions by providing AI technologies" at the edge. Its focus on supporting mission-critical services underscores the understanding that this localised intelligence is crucial for reliable, high-stakes applications.

This holistic view, which integrates network intelligence with edge deployment, is further developed in other ITU-T recommendations. For example, Recommendation ITU-T Y.4122 [167] specifies the requirements and capability framework for an "edge-computing-enabled gateway" on the IoT. This standard recognises that edge gateways in IoT systems must support not only connectivity but also intelligence, providing computation and data processing near IoT devices.

Furthermore, the ITU-T addresses the application of IEC in specific vertical domains. Recommendation ITU-T X.1384 provides security requirements and guidelines specifically for vehicular edge computing (VEC). It analyses the unique threats associated with deploying AI-driven services for intelligent transport systems at the edge and provides the necessary security requirements to ensure their safe deployment. This work demonstrates a clear understanding that the combination of AI and edge computing requires domain-specific considerations for safety and security.

In addition to its technical work, the ITU-T also considers the broader impacts of AI [60]. Its journal has explored the topic of sustainable AI at the network edge, investigating innovations for energy efficiency through hardware-software co-design, energy-aware decision-making, and sustainable AI applications [168]. This reflects a growing awareness that the widespread deployment of AI, particularly at the edge, must be balanced with environmental considerations. Through these combined efforts, the ITU-T is building a comprehensive framework for integrating intelligence into the core and edge of global telecommunication networks.

7.1.5 CEN-CENELEC: Harmonising Standards for the European AI Act

The work of CEN and CENELEC in the field of AI is unique among SDOs as the activities of JTC 21 are driven by a top-down regulatory mandate. The goal is to develop European standards in support of EU legislation as illustrated in Figure 7.1 [143].

The CEN-CENELEC Joint Technical Committee 21 (JTC 21) was established with the specific purpose of developing the technical standards needed to support the European Union's AI Act [126, 169]. This makes JTC 21 a critical instrument of public policy, tasked with translating the legal requirements of the world's first comprehensive AI regulation into practical, implementable technical specifications for industry.

7.1.5.1 A Mandate for Harmonised Standards

The work of CEN-CENELEC JTC 21 is inscribed within a particular regulatory framework at EU level that aims to harmonise essential product requirements across EU Member States. For this purpose, Regulation (EU) No. 1025/2012 empowers the European Commission to request the drawing up of European harmonised Standards ('hENs') by ESOs [127]. These standards shall address essential product requirements and may be applied

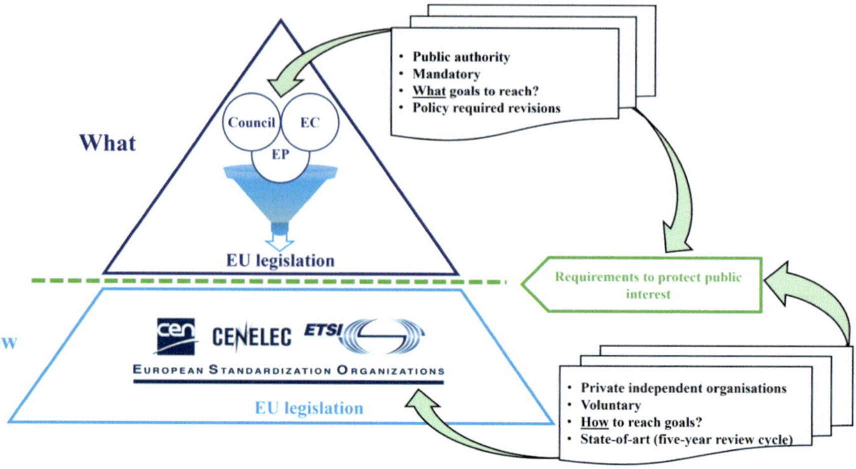

Figure 7.1 European standards in support of EU legislation [143, 69].

alongside relevant product legislation. This regulatory framework recognises, inter alia, the importance of market-driven processes taking place within ESOs and expert consensus for the implementation of EU product legislation.[1]

The power conferred upon the Commission under the Artificial Intelligence Act ('AIA') to request the development of hENs is an application of this regulatory framework.[2] It is against this regulatory background that the Commission has issued a standardisation request to the CEN-CENELEC in May 2023 for the drafting of European standards and standardisation deliverables covering all the essential requirements applicable to high-risk AI systems, AI providers' quality management systems and conformity assessments for AI systems [128]. While the preparation of these standards is underway within the JTC 21, none of the requested standard has been formally published at the time of writing.[3]

AI providers may choose to comply with these future standards for demonstrating the compliance of their high-risk AI system with the AIA's

[1] See article 10 of Regulation (EU) No. 1025/2012, stating that 'European standards and European standardization deliverables shall be market-driven, take into account the public interest as well as the policy objectives clearly stated in the Commission's request and be based on consensus'.

[2] See article 40 of Regulation (EU) 2024/1689. See also the developments on that Regulation in section 6.2.

[3] Note that the Commission's standardization request is valid until 28 February 2026.

essential requirements. Doing so will create a presumption of conformity with all or parts of these requirements and, in certain cases, adapt the types of conformity assessment procedure that must be followed [115]. Reliance on these standards remains, however, voluntary and does not exempt AI providers from their responsibility to comply with the regulation's provisions.

These standards should provide a clear and predictable pathway for manufacturers to demonstrate compliance, significantly reducing legal uncertainty and streamlining market access. This process elevates the role of standardisation from a source of best practices to an integral component of the legal and regulatory framework. The development process itself reflects this unique status, involving formal steps such as drafting by technical experts, public enquiry, voting by national standards bodies, and finally, assessment by the Commission and citation in the Official Journal of the European Union, which gives them their legal force.

7.1.5.2 Key Standards for AI Act Compliance

The work programme of JTC 21 is directly structured to address the key requirements laid out in the AI Act for high-risk AI systems. The committee is developing a suite of core standards that provide the operational frameworks needed for compliance. These include a standard for AI Risk Management, which will give a definitive approach for EU organisations. This standard builds upon international work like ISO/IEC 23894:2023, being tailored to the European context by integrating the AI Act's risk classification categories (high-risk, limited risk, minimal risk) and providing detailed assessment templates and mitigation strategies aligned with the regulation [147].

Another critical deliverable is a standard for an AI Quality Management System (QMS) [6, 115, 119]. Article 17 of the AI Act mandates that providers of high-risk AI systems implement a QMS. The JTC 21 standard will provide the technical specifications for such a system. It is expected to build upon the international AI Management System standard, ISO/IEC 42001:2023, but will add specific European requirements related to regulatory reporting, post-market monitoring, and conformity assessment procedures as stipulated by the Act.

These foundational management standards are being supplemented by a portfolio of more specific standards that address other key requirements of the AIA. This includes work on data governance and quality, ensuring that datasets used to train high-risk systems are of sufficient quality to prevent bias and errors. Other projects focus on transparency, with standards for logging to ensure that the operational history of an AI system can be traced and audited; robustness, to ensure systems perform reliably under pressure; and cybersecurity, to protect systems from malicious attacks [115, 119].

7.1.5.3 The Strategy of "Europeanisation"

JTC 21's strategy is to adopt and adapt [119]. The committee actively collaborates with international SDOs, primarily ISO/IEC, through the Vienna Agreement. Its approach is to adopt international standards wherever they are suitable, such as using ISO/IEC 22989:2022 for terminology and ISO/IEC 23053:2022 as the framework for ML systems. This promotes global alignment and prevents unnecessary duplication of effort.

However, where the EU AI Act imposes requirements that go beyond existing international standards-particularly in areas related to fundamental rights, specific high-risk applications, or conformity assessment procedures, JTC 21 is tasked with developing "homegrown" European standards or adapting international ones to fill these gaps. This process of adaptation leads to the "Europeanisation" of global standards. The resulting European standards, such as the forthcoming QMS and risk management standards, will represent a version of the international standards that has been enhanced with additional layers of regulatory rigour. Because the EU is such a significant global market, companies worldwide that wish to sell their AI products in Europe will likely need to adhere to these more stringent, "Europeanized" standards. This has the potential to export European policy and values globally, making the work of JTC 21 a powerful force in shaping the global benchmarks for trustworthy and regulation-compliant AI.

7.1.6 Analysis of the AI and Edge AI Standardisation Domains

The global landscape of AI standardisation is a complex tapestry woven by multiple organisations, each with its philosophy, focus, and constituency. While their efforts are largely complementary, understanding their distinct roles is crucial for navigating this environment. A comparative analysis reveals a logical, multi-layered structure, with different SDOs addressing different levels of the AI technology stack, from foundational principles to network infrastructure and practical implementation. The domain of edge AI highlights this multi-layered approach, as its standardisation is not happening in a single committee but at the convergence of several distinct technological streams.

7.1.7 Comparative Analysis of SDO Philosophies and Focus Areas

The major SDOs have carved out complementary niches, reflecting their institutional histories and expertise. ISO/IEC, through JTC 1/SC 42, operates at the most foundational and horizontal level. Its purpose is to create a stable, globally applicable, and consensus-driven architectural framework for AI [148].

The system of standards approach focuses on defining the core building blocks, terminology, management systems, risk and quality frameworks, and data principles, that apply to all AI systems, regardless of their application domain or deployment environment.

The IEEE takes a more hands-on, engineering-oriented approach. It operates on a dual track: its P7000 series translates high-level ethical principles into actionable design processes for engineers, while its technical committees develop practical, bottom-up standards that solve immediate implementation challenges [152]. The work in standardising toolchains and frameworks for edge AI demonstrates a focus on the "how-to" of building real-world systems [125].

The telecommunications-focused SDOs, ETSI and ITU-T, view AI through the lens of network architecture and management. Their primary concern is not the internal workings of AI models but how to enable, manage, and secure AI-driven services on communication networks. ETSI's work on Multi-access Edge Computing (MEC) is a prime example of standardising the network infrastructure, the "plumbing", to create an open platform for edge AI applications. The ITU-T, meanwhile, focuses on using AI as a tool to manage the network itself, with its vision of "AI-native" networks that are self-optimising and autonomous [161].

Finally, CEN-CENELEC has a unique and highly focused role. Its work in JTC 21 is entirely top-down and regulation-driven, with the explicit mandate to create harmonised standards that provide a presumption of conformity with the EU AI Act [9].

The focus is on translating legal requirements into technical specifications for risk management, quality, and conformity assessment, making it the key SDO for organisations concerned with regulatory compliance in the European market [119].

Table 7.1 provides a comparative overview of the primary focus areas for each of these SDOs, highlighting their key committees and flagship standards or projects.

Table 7.1 Comparative overview of the primary focus areas for each of the SDOs.

Standardisation Domain	ISO/IEC	IEEE	ETSI	ITU-T	CEN-CENELEC
Foundational Concepts and Terminology	**Lead:** JTC 1/SC 42 (ISO/IEC 22989, 23053)	Contributor (P3123)	Adopts/ References	Adopts/ References	**Lead (EU):** JTC 21 (Adopts ISO/IEC 22989)
Risk Management	**Lead:** JTC 1/SC 42 (ISO/IEC 23894)	Contributor (P3396)	Addresses in security context	Addresses in network context	**Lead (EU):** JTC 21 (European AI Risk Mgt. Std.)
Quality and Trustworthiness	**Lead:** JTC 1/SC 42 (ISO/IEC 25059, TR 24028)	Contributor (P3396)	Focus on testing (MTS) & security (SAI)	Focus on QoS	**Lead (EU):** JTC 21 (AI Trustworthiness Framework)
AI Management Systems	**Lead:** JTC 1/SC 42 (ISO/IEC 42001)	Contributor			**Lead (EU):** JTC 21 (AI QMS for Reg. Purposes)
Ethics and Societal Concerns	Contributor (TR 24368, TR 24027 on bias)	**Lead:** P7000 Series (7000, 7001, 7003)	Contributor	Contributor	**Lead (EU):** JTC 21 (Foundational & Societal Aspects WG)
Data Quality and Governance	**Lead:** JTC 1/SC 42 (ISO/IEC 5259 series)	Contributor (P2801 for medical)	Contributor (ISG for AI agents)		**Lead (EU):** JTC 21 (Standards on datasets)
Network Integration and Management		Contributor (2040-2023)	**Lead:** ZSM, ENI	**Lead:** SG13 (FG-AINN, Y.3172)	
Edge AI Platforms (MEC)			**Lead:** ISG MEC (GS MEC 003, 011)	Contributor (Q.5001)	
Edge AI Implementation and Toolchains		**Lead:** C/AISC (P3342), C/SM (P2975.3)		Contributor (IEC use cases)	
Regulatory Compliance (EU AI Act)	Provides foundational inputs		Provides inputs for telecom		**Lead:** JTC 21

7.1.8 The State of Edge AI Standardisation

As the analysis and table indicate, edge AI standardisation is an emerging field that is not being driven by a single, dedicated committee but is instead coalescing from the work of multiple SDOs with different perspectives on what "the edge" is. There are three primary viewpoints shaping the landscape.

First is the Network Edge perspective, led by ETSI and the ITU-T. Here, the edge is a location within the telecommunications network infrastructure. The focus is on standardising platforms like MEC and Intelligent Edge Computing (IEC) to provide the low-latency, high-bandwidth environment that enables real-time AI services. *7* This view is concerned with service delivery, network management, and creating an ecosystem for applications.

Second is the device edge perspective, led by the IEEE. Here, the edge refers to the end-user devices themselves, such as industrial controllers, IoT sensors, or autonomous vehicles [125]. The focus is on the practical engineering challenges of deploying AI models on these resource-constrained devices. Standardisation efforts like IEEE P3342-2023 (toolchains) and P2975.3-2023 (industrial frameworks) are designed to provide developers with the specific tools and software architectures they need to make AI work in these environments [125].

Third is the Foundational Principles perspective, led by ISO/IEC. From this viewpoint, the location of deployment, be it cloud or edge, is secondary to the need for universal principles of governance. The standards for risk management (ISO/IEC 23894:2023), quality (ISO/IEC 25059:2023), and data management (ISO/IEC 5259 series) are designed to be applied to any AI system, providing the essential underpinnings for trustworthiness regardless of where the computation occurs.

These three streams are highly synergistic. An organisation building a sophisticated edge AI product for the industrial sector might use ISO/IEC 42001:2023 to establish its AI management system, follow the guidance in IEEE P2975.3-2023 to design its software framework, use tools compliant with IEEE P3342-2023 to deploy its models, and run its application on a network operator's MEC platform that conforms to ETSI standards. However, a significant gap remains, as noted in the initial analysis: there is no single, unified, and comprehensive set of standards that covers the entire edge AI lifecycle holistically. A key challenge for the future will be the harmonisation of terminology and frameworks across these different perspectives to create a more seamless and less fragmented standardisation environment for the burgeoning edge AI industry.

Based on the analysis and the overview of the AI standards discussed, Table 7.2 lists the primary AI standards and standardisation activities in the standard development organisations mentioned in this chapter.

Table 7.2 Relevant AI standards and standardization activities

ITU-T - International Telecommunication Union - Telecommunication Standardization Sector	
Y.Suppl.63 to ITU-T Y.4000 series	Unlocking the Internet of Things with artificial intelligence: Where we are and where we could be.
CEN-CENELEC - European Committee for Normalization / European Committee for Electrotechnical Standardization	
FG on AI	Focus Group on Artificial Intelligence. It was the first and only contributor on AI topics in CEN and created a set of interesting documents on first ideas on AI (late 2010') later superseded by a CEN/CLC JTC 21 on AI.
JTC 21	Joint Technical Committee 21 "Artificial Intelligence". It identifies and adopts international standards already available or under development from other organizations like ISO/IEC JTC 1 and its subcommittees, such as SC 42 Artificial Intelligence. Furthermore, it focuses on producing standardization deliverables that address European market and societal needs, as well as underpinning EU legislation, policies, principles, and values.
ISO/IEC - International Organization for Standards / International Electrotechnical Commission	
JTC 1/SC 42	Artificial Intelligence. This overarching JTC focuses on different aspects of AI, produces a set of standards (among which the ISO/IEC 8183: Artificial intelligence - Data life cycle framework) and is composed of a set of WGs.
WG 1	Foundational standards.
WG 3	Trustworthiness.
WG 4	Use cases and applications.
WG 5	Computational approaches and characteristics of artificial intelligence systems.
JWG 4	It administers several Joint WGs with other subcommittees e.g., with IEC TC65/SC65A: Functional safety and AI systems.
TR 24027	Information technology - Artificial Intelligence (AI) – Bias in AI systems and AI-aided decision making.
TR 24028:2020	Information technology - Artificial intelligence - Overview of trustworthiness in artificial intelligence [43].
DTR 24029-1	Artificial Intelligence (AI) - Assessment of the robustness of neural networks - Part 1: Overview [139].
AWI 24029-2	Artificial Intelligence (AI) - Assessment of the robustness of neural networks - Part 2: Methodology for the use of formal methods [142].

Table 7.2 *Continued.*

WD 5259-1	Data quality for analytics and ML - Part 1: Overview, terminology, and examples.
WD 5259-2	Data quality for analytics and ML - Part 2: Data quality measures
WD 5259-3	Data quality for analytics and ML - Part 3: Data quality management requirements and guidelines.
WD 5259-4	Data quality for analytics and ML - Part 4: Data quality process framework
WD 5338	Information technology - Artificial intelligence - AI system life cycle processes.
AWI TR 24368	Information technology - Artificial intelligence - Overview of ethical and societal concerns.
AWI TR 24372	Information technology - Artificial intelligence (AI) - Overview of computational approaches for AI systems.
25012:2008	Software engineering - Software product Quality Requirements and Evaluation (SQuaRE) - Data quality model.
WD TS 4213	Information technology - Artificial Intelligence - Assessment of machine learning classification performance [140].
23894:2023	Information Technology – Artificial Intelligence – Guidance on Risk Management.
WD 42001	Information Technology - Artificial intelligence - Management system.
AWI 25059	Software engineering - Systems and software Quality Requirements and Evaluation (SQuaRE) - Quality model for AI-based systems.
ETSI - European Telecommunications Standards Institute	
OCG AI	Co-ordination Group on Artificial Intelligence. It acts as a coordination group for the standardisation activities related to AI handled in the technical bodies and committees and ISGs of ETSI.
ISG ENI	Industry Specification Group Experiential Network Intelligence. It focuses on leveraging AI methods to increase the dynamicity, adaptability and reaction of telecommunication networks and its acting entities, and on the following MARS-related topics: develop standards for a Cognitive Network Management system, incorporating one or more closed control loops; provide a telemetry processing framework that uses context and situation awareness to learn and reason about which data should be collected using what types of processing mechanisms to support information collection and measurement about network performance, network resources and services.
IEEE SA- Institute of Electrical and Electronics Engineers Standard Association	
A-IS	Autonomous and Intelligent Systems. It ensures that every stakeholder involved in the design and development of autonomous and intelligent systems is educated, trained, and empowered to prioritize ethical considerations so that these technologies are advanced for the benefit of humanity.

Table 7.2 *Continued.*

ECPAIS	Ethics Certification Program for Autonomous and Intelligent Systems. It focuses on certification and marking processes that advance transparency, accountability, and reduction in algorithmic bias in (A-IS).
P3333.1.3	Standard for the Deep Learning-Based Assessment of Visual Experience Based on Human Factors.
P3652.1-2020	Guide for Architectural Framework and Application of Federated Machine Learning.
P2805.3	Cloud-Edge Collaboration Protocols for Machine Learning. It specifies the collaboration protocols of enabling ML on the edge computing node with support from industrial clouds and provides implementation reference for ML on lower powered, cheaper, embedded devices.
P2961	Guide for an Architectural Framework and Application for Collaborative Edge Computing. It defines a ML framework that allows a computing task to be decomposed and distributed across edge and cloud nodes, the architectural framework and application guidelines for collaborative edge computing, and provides a blueprint for data usage, ML, and computing collaboration in edge computing environments.

7.2 Spatial Web Standards

The IEEE 2874-2025 "Standard for Spatial Web Protocol, Architecture and Governance" defines the foundational specifications for a reference model of the Spatial Web, a system designed to integrate physical and virtual environments into a globally accessible, interoperable, and governable framework [59]. This standard addresses the convergence of distributed edge technologies, including extended reality (XR), artificial intelligence (AI), autonomous systems, robotics, and the Internet of Things (IoT) to create a cohesive cyber-physical ecosystem [59]. It serves as a foundational standard that defines compliance for subsequent Implementation Specifications and domain-specific architectures.

As a sociotechnical standard, the IEEE 2874-2025 Spatial Web Standard establishes foundational requirements that are implemented through separate Implementation Specifications to address the following key requirements:

- **Semantic Interoperability:** Establish a shared ontological framework for representing and exchanging meaning between human and AI agents within the Spatial Web.
- **System Explainability:** Enable the modelling and representation of intelligent agent activities and decision-making to enhance transparency and accountability.

- **Cross-Domain Interoperability:** Facilitate universal data and model interoperability in the continuum compute to enable collaboration across organizational, network, and jurisdictional boundaries.
- **Regulatory Compliance:** Ensure adherence to diverse local, regional, national, and international regulations, cultural norms, and ethical standards through built-in governance mechanisms.
- **Identity and Access Management:** Implement decentralized authentication and credentialing systems with privacy and security safeguards to enable fine-grained control over system activities and resources.
- **Multi-Scale Cognitive Computing:** Support distributed, multi-agent AI systems operating across various scales of the Spatial Web ecosystem.
- **Polycentric Governance:** Enable flexible, context-specific governance models that can adapt to diverse domains and use cases within the Spatial Web.
- **Hyperspace Representation:** Provide a framework for representing and navigating multi-dimensional spaces, including physical, virtual, and abstract domains.
- **Real-time Interaction:** Support low-latency, high-fidelity interactions between users, AI agents, and digital twins across the Spatial Web.

The IEEE 2874-2025 standard framework encompasses core components including the Hyperspace Modelling Language (HSML), the Hyperspace Transaction Protocol (HSTP), the Universal Domain Graph (UDG) and a governance framework designed to address ethical, legal, and social considerations in AI deployment and autonomous technologies at the edge. These components are formalized through separate Implementation Specifications that define compliance requirements.

7.2.1 HSML

The Hyperspace Modelling Language (HSML) is a human- and machine-readable semantic modelling language and ontology that provides a shared vocabulary for Domains, Entities, Agents, Activities, Credentials, Channels, and Hyperspaces within the Spatial Web. HSML leverages W3C standards (RDF, OWL, SHACL, and others) to express and validate formal statements and updates, enforcing structure and constraints across heterogeneous implementations. It supports multiple spatial or relational structures including topological, metric, cellular, and vector spaces via well-defined hyperspace

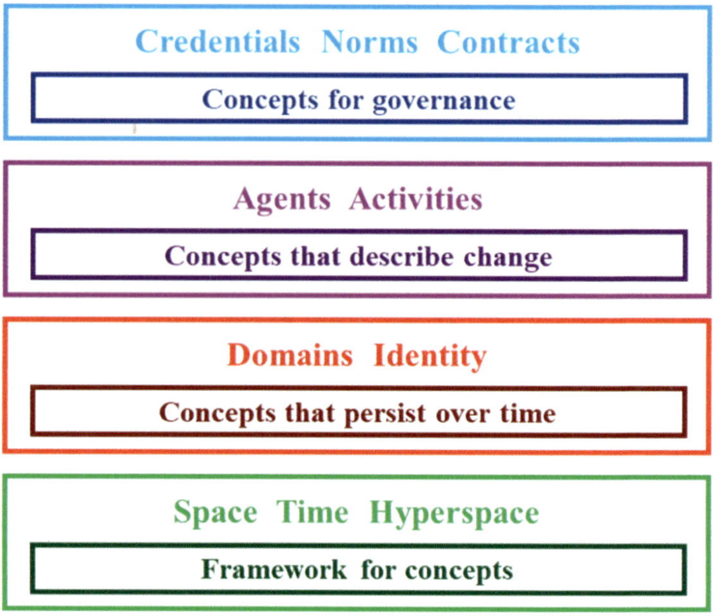

Figure 7.2 HSML knowledge model

constructs such as points, paths, subspaces, tensor products, and structure-preserving morphisms. HSML requires the use of Spatial Web Identifiers (SWIDs) conformant with W3C DID Core for decentralized identity and discoverability. Figure 7.2 illustrates the HSML knowledge model [79].

7.2.2 UDG

The Universal Domain Graph (UDG) refers to the interconnected network of graphs from all domains within both the physical and digital worlds, along with their relationships within the Spatial Web ecosystem. A domain is defined as an entity with a persistent Spatial Web Identifier (SWID) endowed with specific rights and credentials over time. A Domain Authority is an entity credentialed to define the norms and terms governing actors, actions, and credentials within that domain's scope. The UDG comprises nodes representing entities and edges representing the semantic relationships between these entities. The UDG serves as distributed discovery and state management infrastructure, functioning as a critical component for enabling cross-domain semantic interoperability across the global Spatial Web [79].

7.2.3 HSTP

The Hyperspace Transaction Protocol (HSTP) is an application-layer protocol that enables nodes across the edge-to-cloud continuum to communicate, execute functions, and share HSML-encoded data. HSTP is designed as a generic, generalizable protocol to standardize communication between heterogeneous systems, essential for building a coherent, decentralized, secure, and privacy-respecting Spatial Web. HSTP supports multiple protocol bindings to facilitate communication and data transfer between diverse edge and cloud systems in various deployment contexts. By providing a standard semantic layer above these protocol bindings, HSTP enables compliant systems to communicate effectively regardless of underlying transport mechanisms. HSTP sends messages as HSTP Operations, which are transmitted over transport protocols. These requests and responses are encoded using profile encoding formats (JSON, JSON-LD, OData, GraphQL) as specified in the HSML Implementation Specification [79].

7.2.4 Governance

The governance framework addresses the critical need for machine-readable and machine-executable representation of rules, regulations, and policies within Spatial Web domains. Traditional regulatory approaches have been designed solely for human interpretation, with limited consideration for automated compliance by AI systems and autonomous technologies. The Spatial Web governance framework bridges this gap by enabling both human and machine interpretation of the same regulatory structures, ensuring consistent adherence to rules across human and AI actors.

To enable effective governance of rules and policies, the Spatial Web is organized in a hierarchical, nested architecture where policies and rules are inherited from higher jurisdictional levels and cascaded down to edge systems, following established precedence relationships between different governance levels. Domain Authorities define the norms and terms for creating contracts within their jurisdictional scope, establishing governance for actors, actions, and credentials. This hierarchical structure, combined with the Spatial Web's support for heterarchical and nested domain relationships, enables polycentric governance models that can adapt to diverse regulatory contexts while maintaining coherence across overlapping authorities.

This governance structure enables real-time policy updates from regulatory authorities, allowing edge-deployed systems and autonomous agents to adapt dynamically to changing conditions such as environmental factors, security threats, or operational requirements. The framework provides specifications and tools for industry stakeholders and regulatory bodies to create, govern, and manage domain-specific implementations while ensuring compliance with broader jurisdictional requirements [79].

7.3 AI and Edge AI Standardisation Future Outlook

The international and European standardisation landscape for Artificial Intelligence is a dynamic and rapidly evolving domain, shaped by the dual forces of profound technological advancement and pressing regulatory demand. The collective work of ISO, IEC, IEEE, ITU-T, ETSI, and CEN-CENELEC has resulted in a multi-layered and largely complementary framework that provides the foundational principles, practical tools, and infrastructure specifications needed to guide the development of trustworthy AI. The landscape has matured from defining concepts to building operational frameworks for governance, risk, and quality, a shift driven by the widespread deployment of AI and the legal imperatives of frameworks like the EU AI Act.

Our analysis reveals that the SDOs have successfully carved out distinct yet synergistic niches. ISO/IEC provides the universal, horizontal foundation for AI governance. IEEE focuses on translating ethical principles into engineering practice and solving specific implementation challenges, particularly at the device edge. ETSI and ITU-T are building the network-centric infrastructure required for high-performance AI and edge AI services. Finally, CEN-CENELEC serves the critical function of translating European regulations into harmonised technical standards, creating a clear path to compliance.

While significant progress has been made, the standardisation journey is far from over, and several challenges and future directions are apparent. The most critical challenge, especially for the nascent field of edge AI, is harmonisation. With different SDOs approaching the "edge" from network, device, and foundational perspectives, there is a risk of creating a fragmented landscape with conflicting terminology and overlapping frameworks. Continued and deepened collaboration between these bodies will be essential to ensure the development of a coherent and interoperable set of global standards.

The relentless pace of technological innovation presents another challenge. The rise of Generative AI and Large Language Models (LLMs) introduces new and complex issues related to quality, safety, transparency, and evaluation that existing standards may not fully address.1 SDOs will need to be agile in developing new standards and guidance to tackle the unique risks and opportunities presented by these powerful technologies. This will require new metrics and measures, new testing methodologies, and even new quality characteristics beyond those currently defined.

As organisations adopt these standards, there will be a growing need for clear pathways to demonstrate compliance and maturity. The development of AI engineering maturity models, like the Capability Maturity Model Integration (CMMI) in software engineering, could provide a valuable tool for organisations to improve their AI governance and development processes progressively. Furthermore, certification against standards like ISO/IEC 42001:2023 and programs like IEEE CertifAIEd™ will become increasingly important mechanisms for organisations to build trust and demonstrate their commitment to responsible AI to regulators, business partners, and the public.10

In conclusion, the development of a robust, comprehensive, and harmonised body of international standards is indispensable for fostering a global AI ecosystem that is not only innovative and economically vibrant but also safe, reliable, and aligned with fundamental human values. The work of the SDOs analysed in this report forms the essential bedrock for achieving this future, providing the common language and shared principles necessary to navigate the complexities of the artificial intelligence era.

8

Conclusion

This work explores functional and non-functional requirements for edge AI systems, providing a comprehensive framework for understanding and implementing these advanced technologies across the micro-, deep-, and meta-edge continuum. It provides a holistic approach to edge AI system development and deployment by intertwining the concepts of dependability and trustworthiness with these requirements.

The shift towards edge AI represents a significant evolution in AI technology, offering solutions to challenges posed by centralised systems, such as latency, bandwidth limitations, and privacy concerns. However, this transition also introduces new complexities and considerations that must be carefully addressed to ensure the successful implementation of edge AI systems.

The detailed examination of functional requirements highlights the critical capabilities for edge AI systems to perform effectively in diverse, often resource-constrained environments. These include real-time processing, energy efficiency, and adaptive learning capabilities. Equally important are the non-functional requirements, which encompass a wide range of quality attributes from reliability and security to more AI-specific considerations like explainability and fairness.

By linking these requirements to the concepts of dependability and trustworthiness, we underscore the importance of creating edge AI systems that are functionally effective, reliable, secure, and aligned with ethical standards and societal values. This approach recognises that the success of edge AI deployments hinges not just on technical performance but also on the ability to build and maintain trust with users and stakeholders.

Discussing KPIs and measurement methods provides practical guidance for assessing and monitoring edge AI systems. This focus on quantifiable metrics and ongoing assessment is crucial for maintaining system performance and adapting to changing requirements over time.

DOI 10.1201/9788743809586-8

The framework presented in this work offers a foundation for future research and development in edge AI. It highlights areas where further innovation is needed, particularly in addressing the unique challenges of edge environments, such as limited computational resources and intermittent connectivity.

Moreover, the emphasis on ethical considerations and alignment with societal values points to the need for ongoing dialogue between technologists, policymakers, and the public. Ensuring their trustworthiness and societal acceptance will be important as edge AI systems become more prevalent in critical applications.

The international standardisation landscape for AI is dynamic and rapidly maturing. Led by key organisations like ISO/IEC, IEEE, ITU-T, ETSI, and CEN-CENELEC, a comprehensive framework of standards is emerging to guide the responsible development and deployment of AI and edge AI technologies. These standards provide essential guidance on everything from foundational concepts and data quality to the critical issues of trustworthiness, ethics, and risk management.

While significant progress has been made, the work is far from complete. The continued evolution of AI technology, particularly in areas like generative AI and edge AI, will require ongoing development and harmonisation of standards. Collaboration between the various standards bodies will be crucial to ensure a cohesive and globally relevant framework that can foster innovation while safeguarding against potential harms. For organisations developing or deploying AI, active engagement with and adoption of these standards is both best practice and a strategic imperative for building trust, ensuring compliance, and unlocking the full potential of AI and edge AI.

The comprehensive exploration of edge AI requirements provides a valuable resource for researchers, developers, and decision-makers in the field. Offering a structured approach to understanding and implementing edge AI systems contributes to the responsible advancement of this continuously changing technology. As edge AI continues to evolve, the principles and frameworks outlined in this work will serve as essential guides for creating systems that are not only technologically advanced but also dependable, trustworthy, and aligned with broader societal goals.

This publication is a detailed written study focused on functional and non-functional requirements for edge AI systems to provide an overview of current state of play, concepts, definitions, taxonomy and gaps in the field.

Acknowledgements

This publication has received funding through the projects Horizon Europe dAIEDGE [1] and Chips JU EdgeAI [3]. The Horizon Europe dAIEDGE "A network of excellence for distributed, trustworthy, efficient and scalable AI at the Edge" project is supported under grant agreement No 101120726. The Chips JU EdgeAI "Edge AI Technologies for Optimised Performance Embedded Processing" project is supported by the Chips Joint Undertaking and its members including top-up funding by Austria, Belgium, France, Greece, Italy, Latvia, Netherlands, and Norway under grant agreement No 101097300. Funded by the European Union. Views and opinions expressed are however those of the author(s) only and do not necessarily reflect those of the European Union or the Chips Joint Undertaking. Neither the European Union nor the granting authority can be held responsible for them.

References

[1] dAIEDGE, “A network of excellence for distributed, trustworthy, efficient and scalable AI at the Edge.” https://www.daiedge.eu/.

[2] AI4DI, “Artificial Intelligence for Digitising Industry.” https://www.ai4di.eu/.

[3] EdgeAI, “Edge AI Technologies for Optimised Performance Embedded Processing”, https://edge-ai-tech.eu/.

[4] A. Avizienis, J.-C. Laprie, and B. Randell, “Fundamental Concepts of Dependability.” https://people.cs.rutgers.edu/~rmartin/teaching/spring03/cs553/readings/avizienis00.pdf.

[5] J. C. Laprie, “Dependability: Basic Concepts and Terminology,” Dependability: Basic Concepts and Terminology, pp. 3–245, 1992. https://doi.org/10.1007/978-3-7091-9170-5_1.

[6] European Commission, “AI Act.” https://digital-strategy.ec.europa.eu/en/policies/regulatory-framework-ai.

[7] European Commission, “Proposal for a Regulation laying down harmonised rules on artificial intelligence (Artificial Intelligence Act) and amending certain union legislative acts,” COM(2021) 206 final, April 2021. https://eur-lex.europa.eu/legal-content/EN/TXT/PDF/?uri=CELEX:52021PC0206.

[8] NIST, “AI Risk Management Framework,” Artificial Intelligence Risk Management Framework (AI RMF 1.0), vol. 1, no. 1, Jan. 2023, https://doi.org/10.6028/nist.ai.100-1.

[9] European Parliament. “How standards support Europe’s digital competitiveness”, 2024, https://www.europarl.europa.eu/RegData/etudes/ATAG/2024/766231/EPRS_ATA(2024)766231_EN.pdf.

[10] European Commission, High-Level Expert Group on Artificial Intelligence, “Ethics Guidelines for Trustworthy AI.” April 2019. https://www.aepd.es/sites/default/files/2019-12/ai-ethics-guidelines.pdf.

[11] European Commission, European AI Alliance, “Who Is Winning the AI Race: China, the EU or the United States?” https://futurium.ec.euro

pa.eu/en/european-ai-alliance/open-library/who-winning-ai-race-china-eu-or-united-states.

[12] European Commission, Press release, "Digital sovereignty: Commission proposes Chips Act to confront semiconductor shortages and strengthen Europe's technological leadership." https://ec.europa.eu/commission/presscorner/api/files/document/print/en/ip_22_729/ip_22_729_en.pdf.

[13] RISC-V Europe. https://riscv-europe.org.

[14] Techopedia, "Top 10 Countries Leading in AI Research & Technology in 2025." https://www.techopedia.com/top-10-countries-leading-in-ai-research-technology#:~:text=The%20US%20leads%20the%20way,and%20Canada%20following%20closely%20behind.

[15] AI's Next Leap: 5 Trends Shaping Innovation and ROI. https://www.morganstanley.com/insights/articles/ai-trends-reasoning-frontier-models-2025-tmt#:~:text=The%20to.

[16] European Commission (2018). "Communication from the Commission to the European Parliament, the European Council, the Council, the European Economic and Social Committee and the Committee of the Regions" on Artificial Intelligence for Europe, Brussels, 25.4.2018 COM (2018) 237 final. https://eur-lex.europa.eu/legal-content/EN/TXT/PDF/?uri=CELEX:52018DC0237.

[17] European Commission (2020). "On Artificial Intelligence - A European approach to excellence and trust." White Paper. https://eur-lex.europa.eu/legal-content/EN/TXT/PDF/?uri=CELEX:52020DC0065&from=EN.

[18] European Commission (2021). Commission staff working document. Impact assessment. Accompanying the proposal for a regulation of the European Parliament and of the Council. "Laying down harmonised rules on artificial intelligence (Artificial Intelligence Act) and amending certain union legislative acts." https://eur-lex.europa.eu/legal-content/EN/TXT/PDF/?uri=CONSIL:ST_8115_2021_ADD_3

[19] NIST, National Institute of Standards and Technology. "Framework for Cyber-Physical Systems: Volume 2, Working Group Reports." NIST Special Publication 1500-202, https://nvlpubs.nist.gov/nistpubs/SpecialPublications/NIST.SP.1500-202.pdf.

[20] IEC TC 56. "Dependability." https://tc56.iec.ch/.

[21] ISO/IEC 22989:2022. "Information technology - Artificial intelligence - Artificial intelligence concepts and terminology." https://www.iso.org/standard/74296.html.

[22] M. L. Cummings, "Revising human-systems engineering principles for embedded AI applications," Frontiers in Neuroergonomics, vol. 4, Jan. 2023, https://doi.org/10.3389/fnrgo.2023.1102165.
[23] T. Wang, J. Guo, B. Zhang, G. Yang, and D. Li, "Deploying AI on Edge: Advancement and Challenges in Edge Intelligence," Mathematics, vol. 13, no. 11, pp. 1878–1878, Jun. 2025, https://doi.org/10.3390/math13111878.
[24] K. Ahmad, M. Bano, M. Abdelrazek, C. Arora and J. Grundy, "What's up with Requirements Engineering for Artificial Intelligence Systems?" 2021 IEEE 29th International Requirements Engineering Conference (RE), Notre Dame, IN, USA, 2021, pp. 1-12, https://www.doi.org/10.1109/RE51729.2021.00008.
[25] I. Filippov, "Role of AI in requirements engineering - Xray Blog," www.getxray.app. https://www.getxray.app/blog/ai-in-requirement s-engineering.
[26] D. M. Berry, "Requirements Engineering for Artificial Intelligence: What is a Requirements Specification for an Artificial Intelligence? Available at: https://cs.uwaterloo.ca/~dberry/FTP_SITE/tech.reports /RE4AI_TechReport.pdf.
[27] D. M. Berry, "Requirements Engineering for Artificial Intelligence: What Is a Requirements Specification for an Artificial Intelligence?," Lecture Notes in Computer Science, pp. 19–25, Jan. 2022, https://doi.org/10.1007/978-3-030-98464-9_2.
[28] H. -M. Heyn et al., "Requirement Engineering Challenges for AI-intense Systems Development," 2021 IEEE/ACM 1st Workshop on AI Engineering - Software Engineering for AI (WAIN), Madrid, Spain, 2021, pp. 89-96, https://www.doi.org/10.1109/WAIN52551.2021.00020.
[29] G. Gouveia, J. Alves, P. Sousa, Rui Araújo, and J. Mendes, "Edge Computing-Based Modular Control System for Industrial Environments," Processes, vol. 12, no. 6, pp. 1165–1165, Jun. 2024, https://doi.org/10.3390/pr12061165.
[30] S. Choudhary, V. S, D. D. Bhavani, B. N, M. Tiwari, and S. S, "Edge AI Deploying Artificial Intelligence Models on Edge Devices for Real-Time Analytics," ITM Web of Conferences, vol. 76, p. 01009, 2025, https://doi.org/10.1051/itmconf/20257601009.
[31] S. Lee, "Mastering Trade-off Analysis in Systems Engineering," Numberanalytics.com, 2025. https://www.numberanalytics.com/blog/mastering-trade-off-analysis-in-systems-engineering.

[32] U. -E. -. Habiba, "Requirements Engineering for Explainable AI," 2023 IEEE 31st International Requirements Engineering Conference (RE), Hannover, Germany, 2023, pp. 376-380, https://doi.org/10.1109/RE57278.2023.00058.

[33] U. -E. -. Habiba, J. Bogner and S. Wagner, "Towards Explainability as a Functional Requirement: A Vision to Integrate the Legal, End-User, and ML Engineer Perspectives," 2024 IEEE/ACM International Workshop on Responsible AI Engineering (RAIE), Lisbon, Portugal, 2024, pp. 16-19. https://ieeexplore.ieee.org/document/10669867

[34] L. Bass, P. Clements, and R. Kazman "Software Architecture in Practice, 4th Edition," https://www.oreilly.com/library/view/software-architecture-in/9780136885979/

[35] G. Baxter and I. Sommerville, "Socio-technical systems: From design methods to systems engineering," Interacting with Computers, vol. 23, no. 1, pp. 4–17, Jan. 2011, https://doi.org/10.1016/j.intcom.2010.07.003.

[36] N. Yoshioka, J. H. Husen, H. T. Tun, Z. Chen, H. Washizaki and Y. Fukazawa, "Landscape of Requirements Engineering for Machine Learning-based AI Systems," 2021 28th Asia-Pacific Software Engineering Conference Workshops (APSEC Workshops), Taipei, Taiwan, 2021, pp. 5-8, https://doi.org/10.1109/APSECW53869.2021.00011.

[37] INCOSE, "Systems Engineering Handbook," https://www.incose.org/publications/se-handbook-v5

[38] N. Maleki, B. Padmanabhan, and K. Dutta, "AI Hallucinations: A Misnomer Worth Clarifying," 2024 IEEE Conference on Artificial Intelligence (CAI), Jun. 2024, https://doi.org/10.1109/cai59869.2024.00033.

[39] G. Martínez, J. Conde, P. Reviriego, E. Merino-Gómez, H. J. Alberto, and F. Lombardi, "How many words does ChatGPT know? The answer is ChatWords," arXiv (Cornell University), Jan. 2023, https://doi.org/10.48550/arxiv.2309.16777.

[40] O. Levy, I. Dikman, N. Levy and M. Winokur, "Work in Progress: AI-Powered Engineering-Bridging Theory and Practice," 2025 IEEE Engineering Education World Conference (EDUNINE), Montevideo, Uruguay, 2025, pp. 1-4, https://doi.org/10.1109/EDUNINE62377.2025.10981330.

[41] ISO/IEC 23053:2022. "Framework for Artificial Intelligence (AI) Systems Using Machine Learning (ML)." https://www.iso.org/standard/74438.html.

[42] ISO/IEC TS 5723:2022. "Trustworthiness - Vocabulary." https://www.iso.org/obp/ui/#iso:std:iso-iec:ts:5723:ed-1:v1:en.

[43] ISO/IEC TR 24028:2020. "Information technology - Artificial intelligence - Overview of trustworthiness in artificial intelligence." https://standards.iteh.ai/catalog/standards/iso/232a318a-44eb-42a2-9b73-197a06fd04a1/iso-iec-tr-24028-2020.

[44] ISO/IEC 25002:2024. "Systems and software engineering - Systems and software Quality Requirements and Evaluation (SQuaRE) - Quality model overview and usage." https://www.iso.org/standard/78175.html.

[45] ISO/IEC 25010:2023. "Systems and software engineering - Systems and software Quality Requirements and Evaluation (SQuaRE) - Product quality model." https://www.iso.org/standard/78176.html.

[46] ISO/IEC 25012:2008. "Software engineering - Software product Quality Requirements and Evaluation (SQuaRE) - Data quality model." https://www.iso.org/standard/35736.html.

[47] ISO/IEC 25019:2023. "Systems and software engineering - Systems and software Quality Requirements and Evaluation (SQuaRE) - Quality-in-use model." https://www.iso.org/standard/78177.html.

[48] ISO/IEC 25020:2019. "Systems and software engineering - Systems and software Quality Requirements and Evaluation (SQuaRE) - Quality measurement framework." https://www.iso.org/standard/72117.html.

[49] ISO/IEC 25021:2012. "Systems and software engineering - Systems and software Quality Requirements and Evaluation (SQuaRE) - Quality measure elements." https://www.iso.org/standard/55477.html.

[50] ISO/IEC 25022:2016. "Systems and software engineering - Systems and software quality requirements and evaluation (SQuaRE) - Measurement of quality in use." https://www.iso.org/standard/35746.html.

[51] ISO/IEC 25023:2016. "Systems and software engineering - Systems and software Quality Requirements and Evaluation (SQuaRE) - Measurement of system and software product quality." https://www.iso.org/standard/35747.html.

[52] ISO/IEC 25024:2015. "Systems and software engineering - Systems and software Quality Requirements and Evaluation (SQuaRE) - Measurement of data quality." https://www.iso.org/standard/35749.html.

[53] ISO/IEC 25030:2019. "Systems and software engineering - Systems and software Quality Requirements and Evaluation (SQuaRE) -

Quality requirements framework." https://www.iso.org/standard/72116.html.
[54] IEEE 830-1998. "IEEE Recommended Practice for Software Requirements Specifications." https://ieeexplore.ieee.org/document/720574.
[55] ISO/IEC/IEEE 29148:2018. "Systems and software engineering - Life cycle processes - Requirements engineering." https://www.iso.org/standard/72089.html.
[56] ISO/IEC/IEEE 12207:2017. "Systems and software engineering - Software life cycle processes." https://www.iso.org/standard/63712.html.
[57] ISO/IEC/IEEE 15288:2023. "Systems and software engineering - System life cycle processes." https://www.iso.org/standard/81702.html.
[58] ISO/IEC/IEEE 15289:2019. "Systems and software engineering - Content of life-cycle information items (documentation)." https://www.iso.org/standard/74909.html.
[59] ISO/IEC/IEEE 21840:2019. "Systems and software engineering - Guidelines for the utilization of ISO/IEC/IEEE 15288 in the context of system of systems (SoS)." https://www.iso.org/standard/71956.html.
[60] ITU-T - Suppl 72 to ITU-T Y-3000. "Artificial Intelligence Standardization Roadmap." https://www.itu.int/ITU-T/workprog/wp_item.aspx?isn=18060.
[61] M. A. Boden, "Artificial Intelligence and Natural Man." New York: Basic Books. 1977. https://archive.org/details/artificialintell0000bode_k9b4/page/n3/mode/2up.
[62] A. Prasad, A.S. Kumar, P. Sharma, I.D. Irawati, D.V. Chandrashekar, I.B. Musirin, H.M.A. Abdullah. "Artificial Intelligence in Computer Science: An Overview of Current Trends and Future Directions.". Advances in Artificial and Human Intelligence in the Modern Era (2023), pp. 43-60. https://www.researchgate.net/profile/Priyanka-Sharma-91/publication/373856938_Artificial_Intelligence_in_Computer_Science_An_Overview_of_Current_Trends_and_Future_Directions/links/651678cf1e2386049de30bd6/Artificial-Intelligence-in-Computer-Science-An-Overview-of-Current-Trends-and-Future-Directions.pdf.
[63] D.S. Schiff, A. Ayesh, L. Musikanski, and J.C. Havens, IEEE 7010: "A New Standard for Assessing the Well-being Implications of Artificial Intelligence." 2020 IEEE International Conference on Systems, Man, and Cybernetics (SMC), 2746-2753, 2020, https://doi.org/10.1109/SMC42975.2020.9283454.

[64] P. Stone, R. Brooks, E. Brynjolfsson, R. Calo, O. Etzioni, G. Hager, J. Hirschberg, S. Kalyanakrishnan, E. Kamar, S. Kraus, K. Leyton-Brown, D. Parkes, W. Press, A. Saxenian, J. Shah, M. Tambe, and A. Teller, 2016. "Artificial Intelligence and Life in 2030. One Hundred Year Study on Artificial Intelligence." Stanford University, Stanford, CA. https://ai100.stanford.edu/sites/g/files/sbiybj18871/files/media/file/ai100report10032016fnl_singles.pdf.

[65] R. S. Sutton, John McCarthy's "Definition of Intelligence", Journal of Artificial General Intelligence 11(2) 66-67, 2020. https://doi.org/10.2478/jagi-2020-0003.

[66] A. Theben, L. Gunderson, L., López Forés, G. Misuraca, F. Lupiáñez Villanueva. "Challenges and limits of an open-source approach to Artificial Intelligence," study for the Special Committee on Artificial Intelligence in a Digital Age (AIDA), Policy Department for Economic, Scientific and Quality of Life Policies, European Parliament, Luxembourg. https://www.europarl.europa.eu/RegData/etudes/STUD/2021/662908/IPOL_STU(2021)662908_EN.pdf.

[67] N. J. Nilsson. "The Quest for Artificial Intelligence. A History of Ideas and Achievements." Cambridge University Press, 2010. https://ai.stanford.edu/~nilsson/QAI/qai.pdf.

[68] S. Russell and P. Norvig, "Artificial Intelligence a Modern Approach Third Edition," 2010. https://people.engr.tamu.edu/guni/csce625/slides/AI.pdf

[69] O. Vermesan, F. Pétrot, M. Coppola, M. Schneider, and A. Hÿoß. "Industrial AI Technologies for Next-Generation Autonomous Operations with Sustainable Performance", in O. Vermesan and M. Diaz Nava, (eds.) "Intelligent Edge-Embedded Technologies for Digitising Industry,", pp. 1–71, Jan. 2022. https://www.riverpublishers.com/pdf/ebook/chapter/RP_9788770226103C1.pdf.

[70] O. Vermesan, C. De Luca, R. John, M. Coppola, B. Debaillie, and G. Urlini. "Ethical Considerations and Trustworthy Industrial AI Systems" in O. Vermesan and M. Diaz Nava, (eds.) "Intelligent Edge-Embedded Technologies for Digitising Industry," pp. 241–269, Jan. 2022. https://www.riverpublishers.com/pdf/ebook/chapter/RP_9788770226103C9.pdf.

[71] O. Vermesan, M. Coppola, R. John, C. De Luca, R. Bahr, and G. Urlini, "Current Challenges of AI Standardisation in the Digitising Industry." in O. Vermesan and M. Diaz Nava, (eds.) "Intelligent Edge-Embedded Technologies for Digitising Industry," pp. 271–299,

Jan. 2022. https://www.riverpublishers.com/pdf/ebook/chapter/RP_9788770226103C10.pdf.

[72] O. Vermesan, V. Piuri, F. Scotti, A. Genovese, R. D. Labati, P. Coscia, "Explainability and Interpretability Concepts for Edge AI Systems", in O. Vermesan and D. Marples, (eds.) "Advancing Edge Artificial Intelligence," pp. 197-227. https://doi.org/10.1201/9781003478713-9.

[73] R. V. Yampolskiy. "On Defining Differences between Intelligence and Artificial Intelligence." Journal of Artificial General Intelligence 11(2) 68-70, 2020. https://doi.org/10.2478/jagi-2020-0003.

[74] P. Wang. "On Defining Artificial Intelligence." Journal of Artificial General Intelligence, 10(2):1–37. 2019. https://intapi.sciendo.com/pdf/10.2478/jagi-2019-0002.

[75] O. Vermesan, F. Pétrot, M. Coppola, M. Schneider, and A. Hö̈ß, "Industrial AI Technologies for Next-Generation Autonomous Operations with Sustainable Performance." In: O. Vermesan and M. Diaz Nava, (eds.) "Intelligent Edge-Embedded Technologies for Digitising Industry", pp. 1-71. https://www.riverpublishers.com/pdf/ebook/chapter/RP_9788770226103C1.pdf.

[76] Electronic Components and Systems (ECS). "Strategic Research and Innovation Agenda 2024," ECS-SRIA. https://ecssria.eu/ECS-SRIA-2024.pdf.

[77] K. J. Friston et al., "Designing ecosystems of intelligence from first principles," *Collective intelligence*, vol. 3, no. 1, Jan. 2024, https://doi.org/10.1177/26339137231222481.

[78] IEEE SA. "The IEEE Global Initiative 2.0 on Ethics of Autonomous and Intelligent Systems." https://standards.ieee.org/industry-connections/activities/ieee-global-initiative/

[79] Spatial Web Foundation. https://spatialwebfoundation.org/

[80] IEEE SA. "IEEE P2874 Spatial Web, Architecture and Governance Working Group." https://sagroups.ieee.org/2874/.

[81] OECD, "Explanatory memorandum on the updated OECD definition of an AI system." OECD Artificial Intelligence Papers, No. 8, OECD Publishing, Paris, 2024. https://doi.org/10.1787/623da898-en

[82] OECD AI Principles overview. https://oecd.ai/en/ai-principles.

[83] European Commission. "Open access." https://research-and-innovation.ec.europa.eu/strategy/strategy-2020-2024/our-digital-future/open-science/open-access_en.

[84] Open Research Europe. "Data guidelines." https://open-research-europe.ec.europa.eu/for-authors/data-guidelines.
[85] GO FAIR. "FAIR principles." https://www.go-fair.org/fair-principles.
[86] Technology Review. "We finally have a definition for open-source AI." https://www.technologyreview.com/2024/08/22/1097224/we-finally-have-a-definition-for-open-source-ai.
[87] Open Source Initiative. https://opensource.org/osd.
[88] Open Source Hardware Association (OSHWA). https://www.oshwa.org/.
[89] Open Source Initiative. "Open-source AI definition". https://opensource.org/ai/open-source-ai-definition
[90] Ubotica Technologies. "Successful launch of ground-breaking AI-enabled Earth observation satellite." https://ubotica.com/successful-launch-of-ground-breaking-ai-enabled-earth-observation-satellite.
[91] J. Ruiz-Santaquiteria, J. D. Muñoz, F. J. Maigler, O. Deniz, and G. Bueno. "Firearm-related action recognition and object detection dataset for video surveillance systems." Vol. 52, Feb. 2024, 110030. https://doi.org/10.1016/j.dib.2024.110030.
[92] Deloitte. "Stakeholder collaboration in the AI era." https://www2.deloitte.com/us/en/pages/consulting/articles/stakeholder-collaboration-in-the-ai-era.html
[93] European Parliament, "Challenges and limits of an open source approach to Artificial Intelligence". https://www.europarl.europa.eu/RegData/etudes/STUD/2021/662908/IPOL_STU(2021)662908_EN.pdf
[94] TensorFlow. https://www.tensorflow.org
[95] PyTorch. https://pytorch.org/
[96] Keras. https://keras.io/
[97] Hugging Face. https://huggingface.co
[98] OpenCV. https://github.com/opencv
[99] Farama Foundation. "Gymnasium." https://github.com/Farama-Foundation/Gymnasium
[100] Jetson Stats. https://github.com/rbonghi/jetson_stats
[101] Xilinx. "Analytics and machine learning." https://www.xilinx.com/applications/industrial/analytics-machine-learning.html
[102] Eyes of Things. https://eyesofthings.eu
[103] RISC-V. https://riscv.org
[104] BeagleBoard. https://www.beagleboard.org
[105] Raspberry Pi. https://opensource.com/resources/raspberry-pi

[106] Olimex. "Open-source hardware." https://www.olimex.com/Products/IoT/ESP32/ESP32-EVB/open-source-hardware
[107] Antmicro. "Open-source Jetson baseboard." https://antmicro.com/platforms/open-source-jetson-baseboard.
[108] OpenAI. https://openai.com/index/openai-lp.
[109] Regulation (EU) 2016/679 of 27 April 2016 on the protection of natural persons with regard to the processing of personal data and on the free movement of such data, and repealing Directive 95/46/EC (General Data Protection Regulation, GDPR), 2016. https://eur-lex.europa.eu/eli/reg/2016/679/oj/eng.
[110] OECD Privacy Principles. https://www.oecd.org/en/topics/sub-issues/privacy-principles.html.
[111] NIST Privacy Framework. https://www.nist.gov/privacy-framework.
[112] Fair Information Practice Principles (FIPPs). https://www.fpc.gov/resources/fipps/.
[113] EDPB, Opinion 28/2024 on certain data protection aspects related to the processing of personal data in the context of AI models, 2024. https://www.edpb.europa.eu/system/files/2024-12/edpb_opinion_202428_ai-models_en.pdf
[114] EDPB, Report of the work undertaken by the ChatGPT Taskforce, 2024. https://www.edpb.europa.eu/system/files/2024-05/edpb_20240523_report_chatgpt_taskforce_en.pdf.
[115] Regulation (EU) 2024/1689 of the European Parliament and of the Council of 13 June 2024 laying down harmonised rules on artificial intelligence and amending Regulation (EC) No 300/2008, (EU) No 167/2013, (EU) 2018/858, (EU) 2018/1139 and (EU) 2019/2144 and Directives 2014/90/EU, (EU) 2016/797 and (EU) 2020/1828 (Artificial Intelligence Act, AIA), 2024. https://eur-lex.europa.eu/eli/reg/2024/1689/oj/eng.
[116] European Commission, The EU Artificial Intelligence Act. Up-to-date developments and analyses of the EU AI Act. https://artificialintelligenceact.eu/.
[117] European Commission, Approval of the content of the draft Communication from the Commission – Commission Guidelines on the definition of an artificial intelligence system established by Regulation (EU) 2024/1689 (AI Act), 2025. https://digital-strategy.ec.europa.eu/en/library/commission-publishes-guidelines-ai-system-definition-facilitate-first-ai-acts-rules-application.

[118] European Commission, "Approval of the content of the draft Communication from the Commission – Commission Guidelines on prohibited artificial intelligence practices established by Regulation (EU) 2024/1689 (AI Act)", Brussels, 2025. https://digital-strategy.ec.europa.eu/en/library/commission-publishes-guidelines-prohibited-artificial-intelligence-ai-practices-defined-ai-act.

[119] CEN-CENELEC, "Artificial Intelligence.". https://www.cencenelec.eu/areas-of-work/cen-cenelec-topics/artificial-intelligence/.

[120] European Commission, "Third Draft of the General-Purpose AI Code of Practice published, written by independent experts." [Online]. Accessed 10 July 2025. https://digital-strategy.ec.europa.eu/en/library/third-draft-general-purpose-ai-code-practice-published-written-independent-experts.

[121] Regulation (EU) 2023/2854 of the European Parliament and of the Council of 13 December 2023 on harmonised rules on fair access to and use of data and amending Regulation 2017/2394 and Directive 2020/1818 (Data Act, DA), 2023. https://eur-lex.europa.eu/eli/reg/2023/2854/oj/eng

[122] Regulation (EU) 2022/1925 of the European Parliament and of the Council of 14 September 2022 on contestable and fair markets in the digital sector and amending Directives (EU) 2019/1937 and (EU) 2020/1828 (Digital Markets Act). See also European Commission, "Gatekeepers." [Online]. Accessed 10 July 2025. https://digital-markets-act.ec.europa.eu/gatekeepers_en.

[123] Regulation (EU) 2024/2847 of the European Parliament and of the Council of 23 October 2024 on horizontal cybersecurity requirements for products with digital elements and amending Regulations (EU) No 168/2013 and (EU) No 2019/1020 and Directive (EU) 2020/1828 (Cyber Resilience Act), 2024. https://eur-lex.europa.eu/eli/reg/2024/2847/oj/eng

[124] L. Belkadi, "Regulation (EU) 2024/2847 on horizontal cybersecurity requirements for products with digital elements ("Cyber Resilience Act")." *Forthcoming in the Revue du Droit des Technologies de l'Information.*

[125] IEEE P3342-2023. "Standard for Functional Requirements of Toolchain for Artificial Intelligence Model Deployment on Edge Devices, https://standards.ieee.org/ieee/3342/11221/.

[126] CEN-CENELEC. European AI Standardisation, CEN-CENELEC JTC 21, https://jtc21.eu/.

[127] Regulation (EU) No 1025/2012 of the European Parliament and of the Council of 25 October 2012 on European standardisation, amending Council Directives 89/686/EEC and 93/15/EEC and Directives 94/9/EC, 94/25/EC, 95/16/EC, 97/23/EC, 98/34/EC, 2004/22/EC, 2007/23/EC, 2009/23/EC and 2009/105/EC of the European Parliament and of the Council and repealing Council Decision 87/95/EEC and Decision No 1673/2006/EC of the European Parliament and of the Council, 2012. https://eur-lex.europa.eu/legal-content/EN/TXT/?uri=CELEX%3A32012R1025.

[128] Commission Implementing Decision of 22.5.2023 on a standardisation request to the European Committee for Standardisation and the European Committee for Electrotechnical Standardisation in support of Union policy on artificial intelligence and its Annex, C(2023) 3215 final. Accessible at https://ec.europa.eu/transparency/documents-register/detail?ref=C(2023)3215&lang=en.

[129] M. Wagner, M. Borg and P. Runeson, "Navigating the Upcoming European Union AI Act," in IEEE Software, vol. 41, no. 1, pp. 19-24, Jan.-Feb. 2024, https://doi.org/10.1109/MS.2023.3322913.

[130] SEI, Architecting the Future of Software Engineering: A National Agenda for Software Engineering Research & Development, 2021, https://insights.sei.cmu.edu/documents/1308/2021_014_001_741195.pdf.

[131] J. Bosch, H. H. Olsson, B. Brinne and I. Crnkovic, "AI Engineering: Realizing the Potential of AI," in IEEE Software, vol. 39, no. 6, pp. 23-27, Nov.-Dec. 2022, https://doi.org/10.1109/MS.2022.3199621.

[132] A. Simonetta, M. Paoletti, and T. Nakajima, "The SQuaRE Series as a Guarantee of Ethics in the Results of AI systems." https://ceur-ws.org/Vol-3612/IWESQ_2023_Paper_03.pdf.

[133] A. Trenta, Accounting AI Measures as ISO/IEC 25000 Standards Measures, APSEC IWESQ 2023, 2023, https://ceur-ws.org/Vol-3612/IWESQ_2023_Paper_04.pdf.

[134] ISO/IEC 5339:2024. "Information Technology - Artificial Intelligence Guidance for AI Applications," https://www.iso.org/standard/81120.html

[135] ISO/IEC 5338:2023. "Information Technology - Artificial Intelligence - AI System Life Cycle Processes," https://www.iso.org/standard/81118.html.

[136] ISO/IEC 25059:2023. "Software Engineering - Systems and Software Quality Requirements and Evaluations (Square) - Quality Model for AI Systems", https://www.iso.org/standard/80655.html.

[137] ISO/IEC TR 24027:2021. "Information Technology -Artificial Intelligence (AI) - Bias in AI Systems and AI Aided Decision Making," https://www.iso.org/standard/77607.html
[138] ISO/IEC TS 6254:2025. "Information Technology - Artificial Intelligence - Objectives and Approaches for Explainability and Interpretability of ML Models and AI Systems," https://www.iso.org/standard/82148.html
[139] ISO/IEC TR 24029-1:2021. "Artificial Intelligence (AI) - Assessment of the Robustness of Neural Networks - Part 1: Overview", https://www.iso.org/standard/77609.html.
[140] ISO/IEC TS 4213:2022. "Information Technology - Artificial Intelligence -Assessment of Machine Learning Classification Performance," https://www.iso.org/standard/79799.html
[141] ISO/IEC DIS 5259-2:2024. "Artificial Intelligence -Data Quality for Analytics and Machine Learning (ML) -Part 2: Data Quality Measures," https://www.iso.org/standard/81860.html
[142] ISO/IEC 24029-2:2023. "Artificial Intelligence (AI) - Assessment of the Robustness of Neural Networks - Part 2: Methodology for the Use of Formal Methods", https://www.iso.org/standard/79804.html.
[143] C. Kohler and L. Hernalsteen "Drafting Harmonized Standards in support of the Artificial Intelligence Act (AIA)", https://www.cencenelec.eu/media/CEN-CENELEC/AreasOfWork/CEN-CENELEC_Topics/Artificial%20Intelligence/jtc-21-harmonized-standards-webinar_for-website.pdf.
[144] G. J. Soler et al., "Harmonised Standards for the European AI Act," JRC Publications Repository, 2024. https://publications.jrc.ec.europa.eu/repository/handle/JRC139430.
[145] Standard Setting, EU Artificial Intelligence Act, https://artificialintelligenceact.eu/standard-setting-overview/.
[146] Multi-access Edge Computing - Standards for MEC - ETSI, https://www.etsi.org/technologies/multi-access-edge-computing.
[147] G. P. Krog, CEN-CENELEC JTC21 AI Standards: Complete Detailed Overview, 2025. https://jtc21.eu/wp-content/uploads/2025/06/CEN-CENELEC-JTC21-AI-Standards-Complete-Detailed-Overview.pdf.
[148] How the ISO and IEC are developing international standards for the responsible adoption of AI - UNESCO, https://www.unesco.org/en/articles/how-iso-and-iec-are-developing-international-standards-responsible-adoption-ai.

[149] Shaping European Standards Supporting the AI Act - CEN-CENELEC, https://www.cencenelec.eu/news-events/news/2025/newsletter/ots-64-etuc/.
[150] ISO/IEC JTC 1/SC 42 - Wikipedia, https://en.wikipedia.org/wiki/ISO/IEC_JTC_1/SC_42.
[151] CEN/TC 428 N 557 - CEN-CENELEC, https://www.cencenelec.eu/media/CEN-CENELEC/AreasOfWork/CEN-CENELEC_Topics/Artificial%20Intelligence/centc428_whitepaper_aiandictprofessionalism.pdf.
[152] Autonomous and Intelligent Systems (AIS) - IEEE SA, https://standards.ieee.org/initiatives/autonomous-intelligence-systems/.
[153] Artificial Intelligence Standards Committee - IEEE Computer Society, https://www.computer.org/volunteering/boards-and-committees/standards-activities/committees/artificial-intelligence-standards-committee.
[154] IEEE P2975.3-2023 "Recommended Practice for Software Framework for Industrial Artificial Intelligence (AI) At-the-edge," https://standards.ieee.org/ieee/2975.3/11186/
[155] Artificial Intelligence | AI | Standards - ETSI, https://www.etsi.org/technologies/artificial-intelligence.
[156] MEC - ETSI, https://www.etsi.org/committee/mec.
[157] MEC support towards Edge Native Design - ETSI, https://www.etsi.org/images/files/ETSIWhitePapers/ETSI-WP55-MEC_support_towards_Edge_native.pdf.
[158] MEC-Access Edge AI Computing solutions and use cases - AEWIN Technologies, https://www.aewin.com/application/mec-solutions-and-usage/.
[159] New ETSI standard protects AI systems from evolving cyber, https://www.ncsc.gov.uk/blog-post/new-etsi-standard-protects-ai-systems-from-evolving-cyber-threats.
[160] ETSI forms group for AI agents, https://www.eenewseurope.com/en/etsi-forms-group-for-ai-agents/.
[161] ETSI AI Conference 2025 ITU-T SG13 AI Activities and Focus Groups, https://docbox.etsi.org/Workshop/2025/02_AICONFERENCE/SESSION07/ITU-T%20SG13_CARUGI_MARCO.pdf.
[162] Focus Group on Artificial Intelligence Native for Telecommunication Networks (FG AINN) - ITU, https://www.itu.int/en/ITU-T/focusgroups/ainn/Pages/default.aspx.

[163] India Hosts ITU FG-AINN Meeting to Advance AI-Native Telecom Networks - PIB, https://www.pib.gov.in/PressReleasePage.aspx?PRID=2135728
[164] ITU-T Focus Group on "Autonomous Networks" (FG-AN), StandICT.eu 2026, https://standict.eu/standards-repository/itu-t-focus-group-autonomous-networks-fg.
[165] ITU-T Y Suppl. 72 (11/2022) ITU-T Y.3000-series – Artificial intelligence standardisation roadmap, https://www.itu.int/rec/dologin_pub.asp?lang=e&id=T-REC-Y.Sup72-202211-I!!PDF-E&type=items.
[166] Q.5001 - ITU-T Recommendation database, https://www.itu.int/ITU-T/recommendations/rec.aspx?rec=13701&lang=en.
[167] ITU-T Y.4122 (07/2021) Requirements and capability framework of the edge-computing-enabled gateway in the Internet of Things - StandICT.eu, https://standict.eu/standards-repository/itu-t-y4122-072021requirements-and-capability-framework-edge-computing-enabled.
[168] ITU Journal explores sustainable AI at the network edge, https://www.itu.int/hub/2025/07/itu-journal-explores-sustainable-ai-at-the-network-edge/.
[169] CEN and CENELEC launched a new Joint TC on Artificial Intelligence, https://www.cencenelec.eu/news-events/news/2021/briefnews/2021-03-03-new-joint-tc-on-artificial-intelligence/.
[170] ISO/IEC 2382:2015. "Information technology - Vocabulary", https://www.iso.org/standard/63598.html
[171] ISO/IEC 25000:2014. "Systems and software engineering – Systems ans software Quality Requirements and Evaluation (SQuaRE) – Guide to SQuaRE," https://www.iso.org/standard/64764.html
[172] "The ISO/IEC 25000 series of standards," https://iso25000.com/index.php/en/iso-25000-standards
[173] ISO/IEC 23643:2020. "Software and system engineering – Capabilities of software safety and security verification tools," https://www.iso.org/standard/76517.html
[174] ISO 7498-2:1989. "Information processing systems – Open Systems Interconnection – Basic Reference Model. Part 2: Security Architecture," https://www.iso.org/standard/14256.html
[175] ISO 17572-1:2022. "Intelligent transport systems (ITS) – Location referencing for geographic databases. Part 1: General requirements and conceptual model," https://www.iso.org/standard/81955.html

[176] ISO/IEC 27000:2018. "Information technology – Security techniques – Information security management systems – Overview and vocabulary," https://www.iso.org/standard/73906.html

[177] ISO/IEC 29167-19:2019. "Information technology – Automatic identification and data capture techniques. Part 19: Crypto suite RAMON security services for air interface communications," https://www.iso.org/standard/73247.html

[178] ISO/IEC 27036-3:2023. "Cybersecurity – Supplier relationships. Part 3: Guidelines for hardware, software, and services supply chain security", https://www.iso.org/standard/82890.html

[179] ISO 9241-11:2018. "Ergonomics of human-system interaction. Part 11: Usability: Definitions and concepts," https://www.iso.org/standard/63500.html

[180] ISO/IEC 42001:2023. "Information technology – Artificial intelligence – Management system," https://www.iso.org/standard/42001

[181] ISO 9001:2015. "Quality management systems – Requirements," https://www.iso.org/standard/62085.html

[182] ISO/IEC 27001:2022. "Information security, cybersecurity and privacy protection – Information security management systems – Requirements," https://www.iso.org/standard/27001

[183] ISO/IEC 23894:2023. "Information technology – Artificial intelligence – Guidance on risk management," https://www.iso.org/standard/77304.html

[184] ISO 31000:2018. "Risk management – Guidelines," https://www.iso.org/standard/65694.html

[185] IEC 60050-192:2015. "International Electrotechnical Vocabulary (IEV) - Part 192: Dependability," https://webstore.iec.ch/en/publication/21886

[186] IEEE 2874-2025. "IEEE Approved Draft Standard for Spatial Web Protocol, Architecture and Governance," https://standards.ieee.org/ieee/2874/11717/

[187] IEEE 2846-2022. "IEEE Standard for Assumptions in Safety-Related Models for Automated Driving Systems," https://standards.ieee.org/ieee/2846/10831/

[188] IEEE 3652.1-2020. "IEEE Guide for Architectural Framework and Application of Federated Machine Learning," https://standards.ieee.org/ieee/3652.1/7453/

[189] IEEE 7000-2021. "IEEE Standard Model Process for Addressing Ethical Concerns during System Design," https://ieeexplore.ieee.org/document/9536679
[190] IEEE 7001-2021. "IEEE Standard for Transparency of Autonomous Systems," https://ieeexplore.ieee.org/document/9726144
[191] IEEE 7002-2022. "IEEE Standard for Data Privacy Process," https://ieeexplore.ieee.org/document/9760247
[192] IEEE 7003-2024. "IEEE Standard for Algorithmic Bias Considerations," https://ieeexplore.ieee.org/document/10851955
[193] IEEE P7004-2020. "Standard for Child and Student Data Governance," https://standards.ieee.org/ieee/7004/10270/
[194] IEEE P7008-2017. "Standard for Ethically Driven Nudging for Robotic, Intelligent and Autonomous Systems," https://standards.ieee.org/ieee/7008/7095/
[195] IEEE 7009-2024. "IEEE Standard for Fail-Safe Design of Autonomous and Semi-Autonomous Systems," https://standards.ieee.org/ieee/7009/7096/

Index

About the Editors

Ovidiu Vermesan holds a Ph.D. degree in microelectronics and a Master of International Business (MIB) degree. He is Chief Scientist at SINTEF Digital, Oslo, Norway. His research interests are intelligent systems integration, mixed-signal embedded electronics, analogue neural networks, edge artificial intelligence and cognitive communication systems. Dr. Vermesan received SINTEF's 2003 award for research excellence for his work on implementing a biometric sensor system. He is currently working on projects addressing nanoelectronics, integrated sensor/actuator systems, communication, cyber-physical systems (CPSs) and the Industrial Internet of Things (IIoT), with applications in green mobility, energy, autonomous systems, and smart cities. He has authored or co-authored over 100 technical articles and conference papers. He is actively involved in the activities of the European partnership for Key Digital Technologies (KDT) Joint Undertaking (JU), now the Chips JU. He has coordinated and managed various national, EU and other international projects related to smart sensor systems, integrated electronics, electromobility and intelligent autonomous systems such as E3Car, POLLUX, CASTOR, IoE, MIRANDELA, IoF2020, AUTOPILOT, AutoDrive, ArchitectECA2030, AI4DI, AI4CSM. Dr. Vermesan actively participates in national, Horizon Europe and other international initiatives by coordinating and managing various projects. He is a member of the Alliance for AI, IoT and Edge Continuum Innovation (AIOTI) board. He is currently the coordinator of the Edge AI Technologies for Optimised Performance Embedded Processing (EdgeAI) project.

Dr. Alain Pagani is Principal Researcher and deputy director of the Augmented Vision research department at the German Research Center for Artificial Intelligence (DFKI). His research interests include artificial intelligence, computer vision, image understanding, and extended reality. He is the coordinator of the Network of Excellence dAIEDGE about distributed AI at the edge, and the coordinator of the Horizon Europe project CORTEX2 about remote cooperation using extended reality. He is lecturer at the University of Kaiserslautern-Landau, and he has published over 100 articles in conferences and journals. His research finds applications in extended reality for tele cooperation (project CORTEX2), artificial intelligence and computer vision for human-robot cooperation (project FLUENTLY), and artificial intelligence and augmented reality for analysis of extremely large data (project ExtremeXP). Since 2023, he has been a Research Fellow at DFKI, which is a recognition for outstanding scientific achievements and special achievements in technology transfer.

For Product Safety Concerns and Information please contact our
EU representative GPSR@taylorandfrancis.com Taylor & Francis
Verlag GmbH, Kaufingerstraße 24, 80331 München, Germany